T0078371

Why Witches
Are Still Flying
in Africa?

Why Witches Are Still Flying in Africa?

MFUNDO BADELA

PARTRIDGE
A Penguin Random House Company

To order additional copies of this book, contact
Toll Free 0800 990 914 (South Africa)
+44 20 3014 3997 (outside South Africa)
orders.africa@partridgepublishing.com

www.partridgepublishing.com/africa

Contents

INTRODUCTION

Why are witches still flying in Africa? Is this the pertinent question that everybody should be asking? They are flying in a sense that majority of the people still believe in them. The witches are flying inside the heads of the people.

There are numerous reasons and factors that are responsible for this state of affairs. The main reason is traditional beliefs in magic that are embedded in the community and the new beliefs that were introduced by the people from Europe, the Far East and the Middle East, collaborated the existing beliefs in terms of believing in supernatural power. Many people in our country do embrace or are willing to embrace change, progress and development, but humans are humans. There will always be those human beings who will not accept change at the expense of what defines them. This is prevalent all over the world in terms of heritage, language, location, culture, beliefs, ethnicity no matter what advantages and benefits the changes may bring to the fore. Instead those changes can be absorbed and be adopted into their own way of life and thinking.

Colonisation in Africa and South Africa did not allow the integration of the different communities due to the separate development system of racial and tribal segregation policies of the colonial masters. Coincidentally, they themselves were preserving their heritage, culture, and so on resulting in more than one nation in one country the whites, the Coloureds, the Indians and blacks with different tribes among the black race. Even before the Europeans graced the African shores the blacks especially in Southern Africa were not living together as one nation, instead they were geographically sparse according to their tribes/clans, even fighting among each other for different reasons. It would be disingenuous to blame colonisation and apartheid alone in separating the African tribes, it is just that this separation was an added advantage to them and it made things simple for the Europeans when ruling South Africa to invoke this indigenous separation. This system naturally ensures that the status quo remains, there is little or no intermingle of cultures.

Let me give just a practical example. Different races and tribes have been living in one country being South Africa for so many years, but only few of them speak one another languages voluntarily due to segregation, this ensured that there is no common culture we can identify with. Even among the indigenous Africans themselves many do not understand one another's language except at least those living in urban centres where there is some mixture of races and tribes. So the way of life of the indigenous population, which is characterised by adherence to customs, traditions, culture and beliefs was not disturbed so much especially in their original locations. Even if they were removed, they were removed entirely to a new area without mixing with anybody other than their own clan this guaranteed the keeping of their culture, traditions, and beliefs.

Just imagine in that situation. If someone introduces new things, those things will be turned into local flavours, needs etc. Even myself, I was not immune. My rural home district of Herschel in the province of the Eastern Cape is dominated by AmaHlubi ethnic group that I belong to. I know some who permanently settled into our area from other ethnic groups, had discarded their cultures and adopted ours. The self-governance of each ethnic group promoted nationalism and pride in that certain community and there was a sense to preserve and respect the heritage of their forefathers. Any foreign culture or belief that is introduced must have to conform to the existing beliefs and cultures, so addition rather than subtraction was the ultimate winner.

This was the case that led to the naturalisation of Christianity long time ago to fit in with the traditional African belief systems. So was the addition of the pillars of strength against the existing evil called witchcraft, (ubuthakathi) in my IsiXhosa mother tongue. I deliberately use the words *pillar of strength* to demonstrate where the witchcraft belief owes its existence to. First of all, in pre-Christian times, the stance of witch doctors, healers and ancestral belief was against the evil of witches. Without it, they would be useless, there would be nothing to chase away or to justify their existence. Witchcraft too exists because of them. They give strength to the existence of the belief, which is why I call them the pillars of the witchcraft belief.

Christianity was an addition to the stable, and it fitted very well because the only difference between it and the existing local beliefs is that it is in written form, while the local beliefs are passed from generation to generation orally. I have listed the similarities of these beliefs in the subsequent chapters. The pillars are there to support the structure, to make it stand. These pillars are defined in detail in the book.

The witches are still flying at least in our minds. As a consequence, these witches, still flying with brooms inside our heads, are creating an unsafe environment in our community.

Since the nature has created a system that is inescapable by its very nature—duality. Everything has to survive by the mercy of this system. It is highly incomprehensible to just imagine the universe without duality, meaning that everything on the universe has to have its opposite number for example black and white, evil and good, war and peace, tall and short, etc.

Religion too did not escape this duality. This is my main focus in the book. For religion to be religion or for it to exist, it should represent good it should stand on the ground of goodness. Even now, nature dictates that everything has to have its opposite otherwise, there would be no reason for religion to exist anyway. It owes its existence to its archenemy which is evil represented by a witch and satan. It will be unthinkable to remove one part of the duality and leave the other part and think that the other part will survive alone. Ancestral belief and witchdoctors/diviners thrived through the chasing away of witches. Judaism, Christianity and Islam thrived through the chasing away of the mighty Devil, without these targets the above-mentioned beliefs will be completely useless and redundant. If you take evil out of the equation, there is no longer any duality it is highly impossible and unnatural to say the least.

This is tantamount to preaching or teaching that there is no evil. Can you tell a Muslim and a Christian that there is no Satan and they must stop believing in the existence of evil and darkness? The same applies to the ancestral religion and the Africanised Christianity. Preaching and telling them that they must not believe in the existence of witchcraft is like telling them that there is no evil and they must refrain from believing in the existence of evil spirits or forces of darkness. That would be highly impossible and unnatural.

This is the central theme of my first book. South Africa has just defeated the abhorrent crimes against humanity—racism, tribalism and sexism—with the help of the world. Ironically, there has been a silent crime going on alongside the above-mentioned crimes. I am glad it also drew the attention of the UN (United Nations) as the apartheid did. Successive regimes that ruled South Africa, past and present, have been unsuccessful in getting rid of the scourge of witchcraft belief, resulting in gruesome murders of the innocent, false accusations, maiming and displacements. This is due to the negation of the root cause of the scourge of witchcraft belief.

This conundrum needs some guts to eliminate because unfortunately it is tied to the duality of nature that is good and evil. The witchcraft belief which is the representation of evil will not go if the religions that represent good that opposes it are not eliminated too—i.e. Christianity and ancestral belief. At the moment, South Africa is operating on a vacuum in terms of the laws that should outlaw or supress witchcraft belief. All the laws that were promulgated more than a hundred years ago and in subsequent years did not have the desired effects because they were designed to do the impossible—the impossible task of separating or banning the belief in the existence of evil and leaving the belief in the existence of good alone, meaning breaking up the duality of nature i.e. good and evil.

That is why after one hundred and twenty years since the promulgation of the first law to suppress witchcraft belief to date there is no end in sight of the accusations, insults, pinpointing, brutal killings, ritual murders, ripping off of body parts, and stigmas attached to the so-called witchcraft and witches. The problem is that the evil belief they want to suppress is attached to something that enjoys open immunity— the cultures and religions to be specific, traditional African ancestral religion and Christianity.

This should have been the ringing bells for the politicians to recognise that the problem is not going to be solved in the benches by the judges it is a belief problem that needs a different approach and strategy altogether. This is reminiscent of the terrorism that is currently ravaging the human species around the world this scourge was not born out of pure evil it was inspired by religious text. But the politicians are in permanent denials, and the consequences of that is the never-ending bloodshed of innocent civilians.

The scourge of the witchcraft belief did not come out of the blue nor does it survive alone without being attached to religions. It's got roots and pillars that support it. The following are the four pillars that keep witchcraft relevant and seen as reality in South Africa 1. African ancestral belief 2. Churches 3. Witchdoctors 4. Media. This book tries to explain how these pillars are responsible for the persistence of the witchcraft belief myth and also dissects the impasse and offers long-lasting, permanent solutions to this long-lived scourge.

CHAPTER 1

Flying witches of Africa

Living in the land of witches

Is there anyone who ever contemplated or know how to reside in the land of witches? The whole nation is gripped by the fear and reverence of magic. Who would have thought that our beautiful and wonderful land called South Africa have got places designated just for witches. The villages of witches were created as the results of the chasing away of people that are accused of witchcraft by the communities they reside with. Some call these villages refugee camps for witches. These camps are for their own safety together with their families.

In areas that I am familiar with, where witches are prevalent, there are certain areas that are no-go areas during the nights, and there are roads from which you must divert during the night. During the night, if it happens that one have to walk alone back to the house, some people may accompany one because it is said that when you are walking in groups, the evil spirits of witches or witches themselves have no power to approach a group literally, they are afraid of the group. Some people walk alone during the night. But for those who are afraid, it is so because of witches. If certain people give you something, it is not easy or normal just to accept anything you may refuse it just because one is very cautious in relation to witchcraft. It is even worse if one dreams a person he/she suspects or a known witch or somebody related to the witch a dream is taken as the hard evidence of being bewitched, this dream sometimes must have to be interpreted by the witchdoctor, who will obviously confirm the worst fears. My talkative friend from the province of KwaZulu Natal who is older than I whom I used to meet in the gym is running a liquor business in the small industrial park in the south of Johannesburg, recently his business has not been doing well he complained to me that since the people from his original home knew the location of his liquor business, he is no longer making profit those people from his home are bewitching him so that he can lose his livelihood of selling. To be magic minded is not a child's play it is a serious stuff, when in every sphere of life a magic has to be brought in, this has gone too far. As always, every ailment is attributed to witches. In car accidents witches and concoctions are blamed not reckless driving, even strokes and heart attacks are not left out of the magic, heathy lifestyle is not considered whereas magic will be considered. There is nothing called a natural death in witchcraft-minded communities. Every death is treated as the consequence of witchcraft, and the perpetrators are already known the usual suspects of course are old people living nearby. If there are traditional ceremonies in the houses of the so-called witches or their relatives, some may boycott them, citing witchcraft. They fear being sick and not succeeding in life if they eat the meat and drink the home-brewed beer of that particular house in question.

A long time ago in my village, a drunkard man woke up a granny who was also suspected of witchcraft, but she was selling traditional beer. I don't know the reason why he woke her during the night, whether he needed traditional beer or not. Apparently, an argument ensued there, and it reached a point where the old woman picked up a rock and pelted the man with the aim of chasing him away from her homestead. The drunk man did oblige he left that homestead with that rock that was directed at him in his hand. The following day, there was a meeting (imbizo) of the elders of the village to resolve the issue. The man was still carrying that piece of rock to show to the community and for them to be witnesses that if something happened to him, they must realise that the rock that hit him from the hand of the witch had been laden with evil spells and so on.

The fear of coming across witches during the night provided some sort of curfew in our areas, but some people do walk during the night alone especially the drunken fellows. It is much worse when an owl makes some noise during the night since it is well-known as the bird of evil spirits and as a weapon employed by the witches to do their dirty work. No one will dare get out of the house except for those who got some courage, but I have not noticed them. To make matters worse, in rural villages, there are no streets lights it is pitch black. It is really terrifying. The fear that will make people not walk during the night is not that of thugs who would mug, stab or shoot someone or that of a hungry lion roaming the streets. There are no dangerous wild animals and thugs in our areas.

In the adjacent village during the 1980s, there was talk of a very tall object that inadvertently imposed a curfew in that area it was the talk of the surrounding villages. It was said that after eight o'clock in the evening, it was rare to see people loitering. In areas I am familiar with, the only things that are most feared during the nights are the ghosts, witches and their familiars. I remember when we used to attend the witchdoctor's traditional ceremonies during the nights we would walk in groups. We were always ready for anything. Running was our only weapon. If it happened that somebody mistook a shade for something else or see a shrub or a tree shaking, we would run for our lives, in the process some would fall sustaining scratches, some laughing, and so on. When the other boys ran, there was no time to ask because in our minds, there was this fear of coming across a witch, since the nights are known to be their time of flying and so on.

During the nights, we know what to expect or what we must expect, and naturally we are all in fear of that. Some people will even oversleep at the house he/she visited if it happens that the time lapsed and the remaining hours are those of witches and ghosts. This type of restriction does not happen during the day. During the day, everybody is free. You can criss-cross the dusty streets of the villages the way you like, even far-flung or adjacent villages, free of fear because it is known that the witches are resting/sleeping. When night falls, they begin their job of flying and hurting people.

Some folks who work in urban centres are reluctant to go back home to the rural hinterlands for fear of witches. Some are even told by diviners not to shake hands with anybody when arriving home from the big cities, meaning they must not greet or visit some people. Even money can be a curse. Some diviners tell people whenever they arrive at their homes in rural areas they must not give money as gifts to other people. They should rather buy something for that somebody because money can be cursed as a consequence, one may not succeed with his/her money. It will just vanish as if one is not working.

There are some people I know personally who have relocated to other places, running away from the evil of witchcraft. Some urban workers who are on holidays at home will be reluctant to tell even her/his close friends and some members of the family about the date of departure back to the urban centres it is kept a secret with the view of not alerting the witches who may prepare to block them or hurt them.

The land of witches is not without controversy. My family and I were not immune too. All along my granny was called a witch by some people in the village, we just brushed that aside not knowing that those utterances and accusations one day would solidify into a tragedy until that faithful night in the winter of 1996. We were attacked for the same reason witchcraft, and the attack took place at my granny's (not biological) homestead. At that time, there was an initiation ceremony in the family outside of my granny's homestead. As a norm, the winter season is the initiation season in our area, and I myself went there the previous winter. My granny's cousin just across the river visited her to have some tea and chat as a norm before he proceeded to the kraal. Shortly, he joined us in the kraal, where he fell ill, a car was organised to take him to the hospital, where he unfortunately lost his life.

While he was on his way to the hospital, a middle-aged man at that time called for attention in the kraal. We were all ears.

He yelled and lambasted at our village for being witches and wicked, pointing at that incident. My blood started to boil since I had heard that the sick man had been in my granny's house, drinking tea, but I did not see him while he was in my granny's homestead because I was n't there earlier. Thereafter the sad news came of the passing of my granny's cousin, and the news spread like wildfire as usual. The accusation of the tea laden with a potion to kill started doing rounds. It was the talk of the villages. Even us members of the family when one approaches people busy talking they would abruptly cut short their chat, meaning the talk was about this incident. At that time it was not nice at all.

Two days after the incident, the group of men from the area of the deceased attacked the homestead of my grandmother with the aim of eliminating her as she was accused of poisoning the man with a concoction. Fortunately, she was not there at the time of the attack as she was on a church pilgrimage in Port Elizabeth (Nelson Mandela Bay). There was talk of her being on the run. During the attack, my aunt and three female cousins—one was a child at the time—were there. The two cousins were not hurt, but my aunt and the baby used the back window to escape with injuries. They were later taken to the hospital.

The horde of men even tried to burn the houses but to no avail. The incident happened less than an hour after I left the homestead. The following morning, I was going to leave for Johannesburg. I was there to greet them since I was going to catch the early morning bus. It would have been impossible to see them in the morning that's why I went there during the evening. Luckily, there were no fatalities.

Some people in other areas were not so lucky to live to tell the story. The witch hunters were arrested, but to date, there are no convictions—as if this is enough.

Can you believe it, as I said earlier about the witch refugee camps. This is the year 2015, it seems as if the magic is relentless in its pursuit of blinding reality.

This story appeared in *The Sowetan*, a daily newspaper, on April 4 2015. The place is Helena, Limpopo province, which is known as a *baloyi* village (the place of witches). This place has been a haven for many who had escaped the witch-hunts in their communities. Villages like this are real and existing in South Africa. They are refugee camps for the evicted or banished alleged witches and are spread in many parts of the country.

An affected woman said she would never forget how they were singled out as witches. 'We lost everything and had to run,' said the woman. When we tried to go back to look for our cows, they had also been stolen.

This is an age-old tradition of pillaging after witch smelling. Even their children are bullied in schools and are accused of being the children of witches. 'Apparently, this is not the only place where people have been dumped,' said a government official who was working on this problem.

That is how life is lived in areas where witches still fly in the minds of many superstitious fellows. The hurtful stories are endless, the stories can even take half the space for books in the Library of Congress. Tragically, this is the everyday lives of many people in my country. It is not a joke they genuinely believe in this scourge of flying during the night.

Witchcraft a product of ancient beliefs

In my own description, *witchcraft* is the imagined thinking inside the minds of people who were raised and have lived through the indoctrination of non-existent magic into their heads, giving them the impression that things can be achieved and can happen without following conventional means but by following supernatural means.

The *Oxford South African Pocket Dictionary, 2006.* third edition wrongly defines *witchcraft* as 'the practice of magic especially the use of spells and the calling up of evil spirits'.

I do not understand why they wrote this type of fiction because they have not seen anybody calling or able to call evil spirits. How does one call evil spirits? Where are the evil spirits? Have they seen somebody practising witchcraft? These types of explanations are the ones that mislead people to thinking that witchcraft is real. Some of the dictionaries should go back to the drawing board and analyse the meaning of certain words, especially the ancient words.

I told my colleague that for witchcraft to be real, it really needs sophisticated and advanced technology, and by today's standards, it is impossible to achieve. I mean how can a broomstick so light carry a human body for the whole night, flying over the whole village or town? Where does this broomstick obtain energy from? After that, it will be returned to the house intact. Why human beings have allowed themselves to regard this hogwash and nonsense as real and true for centuries?

There are some people who said and are still saying that white people are witches of the day while the blacks are witches of the night. The explanation is simple. We see airplanes take off and land, and we communicate without seeing one another to some people, those are the results of white witchcraft. This also means black people use their black magic for hurting people, not for development or health or creating employment, while the whites are doing good things with their day magic. It is a well-known fact that the black witches cannot bewitch white people; they are impenetrable by nature. Even the witch doctors find it difficult to use their magic herbs and concoctions to go after the white people.

There are differing explanations about this. Some say if somebody does not believe in black magic or is not using the magic herbs, that person is not susceptible to being bewitched. In South Africa there are few whites who consult traditional healers and witch doctors. I do not understand whether this is due to non-belief in traditional ethnic practices or due to centuries-old isolation from black communities. Either way, a majority of them are non-believers in traditional African practices.

In 1995 the provincial government of the then Northern Province (Limpopo) instituted a commission of enquiry into witchcraft and ritual murders that were plaguing the province. It was led by Professor Ralushai, and the commission of enquiry on witchcraft murders in 1995 made findings. One that fascinates me is the following finding about the deepness of the scourge, the authors of the report presented witchcraft beliefs as primordial and invoked the past to explain the present.

The report states, 'Our forefathers regarded witchcraft as an integral part of our lives.' The authors also claimed that 'traditional beliefs moulded Christianity rather than vice versa. Religious teachings reportedly have little impact, and church people still adhere to the traditional beliefs relating to witchcraft and ancestors. Niehaus, 2001. 187, 188).

The situation is exactly the same as of the time I'm writing this book. Firstly, I will start with the root cause of the witchcraft belief, its origins, where it really emanates from because it did not come out of the blue; it has its deeply embedded roots—although we do not acknowledge and accept this fact. The environment is overwhelming; we are talking of dual worshipping. Some Africans families are accommodating god of Abraham and their ancestors, literally mixing the Western religion and the traditional African religion.

I always thought to myself that us in Africa are very unfortunate in relation to spirituality; our colonisers brought an organised written religion that made no difference to our indigenous religion in terms of improbable claims about the origins of life and the universe. All the claims of both religions are easy to debunk by just advancing reason and science. The Western religion did bring literacy, help organise the community, build health centres, fight for justice, and engage many other developmental issues. But the fact remains that their belief and our traditional ancestral worship are groundless, and both of them are based on faith, not facts.

Accordingly, we Africans mingled these two false ancient ideas and in so doing, perpetuated the falsehood for generations. The God of Abraham, ancestors, and witch doctors represent good, and they are all fortresses against evil in other words, they will be rendered redundant if they are not chasing evil. Satan and the witches, their opposite number, represent evil. These five ancient life wreckers have dominated our lives for centuries. People did and still believe in these five false and misleading beliefs as true and existing, in case of witchdoctors they do exist, because they are human beings, but their utterances and predictions are non-existent. Let me list the five myths again; 1. God of Abraham 2. Ancestral worship 3. Witch doctors 4. witchcraft 5. Satan. Out of these five ancient beliefs, we want to pull out, extract, single out, and outlaw only one—witchcraft— because of its fatal consequences directed at our senior citizens.

In 1895 the British colonial regime enacted a law particularly to suppress this belief that is tied to other beliefs, and the Union of South Africa government did some changes in 1957. In 1970 minor changes were made too. In 1995 the Ralushai Commission of Inquiry on witchcraft murders investigated and made recommendations, and lastly in 1997, the Mpumalanga Province enacted the laws against this scourge, but these were put on hold due to court challenges by the interested parties. To date, South Africa has no law that seeks to end the scourge of witchcraft murders. The parliament has tasked the South African Law Reform Commission to attend to this urgent issue.

All the passed laws that were supposed to suppress witchcraft beliefs were repealed due to their ineffectiveness in quelling the problem. Why did all these laws fail? This year 2015, marks 120 years since the first law was enacted, and seemingly, there is no end in sight of the witchcraft murders in South Africa. Then the question is, why for such a long time has the scourge persisted unabated? It can be that the root have never been dug out. It keeps feeding the stem with rich nutrients, the stem flourishes to spit out more seeds that spread out like veld fires, and the seeds turn into roots again—a vicious cycle indeed. The other problem might be that the legislators of the failed laws did not provide the replacement for the belief in the existence witches, because the belief in the existence of Satan was/is not an alternative of the ancestral religion and Africanised Christianity to accept. In other words the legislators were creating a vacuum in belief breaking up a natural duality of good versus evil. That was not going to succeed anyway.

Has anybody asked himself/herself where this belief comes from, where it obtains its strength/survival, what motivates it to last so long with its hallmarks of brutality? Again, what validates and legitimises the scourge? Was Sam Harris right when he said in his book *The End of Faith*, 2006. 89 'Occult beliefs of this sort are clearly an inheritance from our primitive, magic- minded ancestors'. In the Western world and other parts of the world, this dark belief was unceremoniously discarded with the emergence of the Enlightenment Project. Previously, I said why did we dissociate this ancient myth from other ancient myths, and can they be associated? The answer is yes. Why? I have got this to say according to my opinion.

If one believes that Jesus can turn a stone into bread and water into wine, what will make one not believe that a granny across the street can bewitch one's father, causing him to be mad and in addition, that the same granny turned into a black cat during the night? When one's mind is groomed to accept the supernatural as reality, it is easy to accept the preceding fables. Both preceding fables are about non-existent magic. Only the magic minded will see no problem in accepting them.

Again, here's another example. If the God of Abraham can kill many people who apparently disobey his laws by causing a plague, what will make one not believe that an ancestor can make him/her fertile and produce an offspring by not following the conventional means? Reasonably, both of these fables do not make any sense. They are full of improbabilities to say the least. They do not make sense to me and other human beings around the world. But then what about the masses who believe in them? They were indoctrinated and are still being indoctrinated and will possibly continue to be indoctrinated about the supernatural in the foreseeable future. We must remember that early indoctrination reaches deep. It is their way of life. They drink it, sleep it, eat it it is their world view. What makes matters worse is that there is no alternative being put forward to counter these bad and frivolous ideas.

This is reminiscent of the Stone Age, where there were no alternatives and the only explanation was supernatural. Unlike today, we are spoilt with choices on almost everything. I mean, information about our origins and that of the universe is in our fingertips. But why are some of our fellow human beings still trapped in the Stone Age psychologically and spiritually? A bright microbiologist can believe that dead people can influence or change his life or the lives of the nation. A physicist can believe that the angels were created by god from light, in particular angel Gabriel was sent to reveal the word of god to Mohamed. Is this rational? No, they all defy reason.

As far as I am concerned, God, ancestors, Satan, witches, witch doctors—the five elements that are ravaging Africa and the world—are inextricably linked. The biggest mistake that the authorities in South Africa have made in the past and present is in trying to isolate one myth from other myths that gave birth to it. If we are serious about defeating the scourge of witchcraft murders in South Africa (as we had failed dismally in the previous attempts), we have to be sober minded and face the reality. Witchcraft belief did not just pop up on its own. There are natural factors that gave the belief its legitimacy and survival. Interestingly, those factors themselves are based on groundless, unproven, and irrational age-old myths.

Why did the unwanted, dangerous witchcraft belief survive this long? It is because their opposite number also survived this long. If the beliefs in God, ancestors, witch doctors, and in the existence of the devil still thrives, so will the witchcraft belief. If they can vanish into thin air, witchcraft belief will not survive either. I guarantee that. I know witchcraft belief personally. I've lived through it, and now I am observing it. My place of birth, the rural areas of the former homeland of Transkei (now Eastern Cape Province), is the bastion of witchcraft belief. This belief prevails as it is the culture. I also believed in its existence as a norm, but I never saw a witch. The only case I personally know of is that granny in the village who is accused of witchcraft.

Nobody ever caught a witch in my village it was always accusations that resulted in the division of families and community, and apparently, this division is deeply rooted it is hereditary. There are always allegations that a witch passes the baton to her offspring to continue with the job of evil doing and it is gender based. The granny could have taught and trained her daughter and daughter-in-law how to do it, paving the way for them to take over the reins when the old lady left this world. The daughter of this alleged witch also carried this unnecessary burden of being accused as a witch.

While we were growing up, we were told or it was common knowledge in villages even now that that particular house was not a good one and that we must not even play with the children of that family to avoid being bewitched and coming to our homes carrying the bad omen that would destroy our families. If it happened that as a child you ate something given by the family of the suspected witches, you would be rebuked, even whipped. A certain lady was pinpointed as the one who inherited witchcraft from her mother, who was a well-known witch. Well, we did not even know her, the old witch who passed the baton, and she died a long time ago.

The ugly side of this is that it does not only burden the accused the accusers also inherit this culture of accusing from their forebears. The offspring of the accusers will never like the family of the accused, whereas nothing bad happened to them that can be attributed to the accused offspring. The opposing sides will never work together in the community, meaning the witchcraft belief is very divisive among the families and ultimately the community. Some families have reluctantly relocated to other areas due to banishment by the members of the community or for their own safety.

As I said earlier, my own family was also a victim of witch-hunts. We were lucky because there were no fatalities. We are among those few fortunate enough to live and tell the story. We knew everything about the belief all around us, but the physical attack was foreign to us and in our area. It used to be accusations and counter-accusations as usual and the resultant divisions and hatred accompanied by insults and name-calling. We were always hearing and reading about these gruesome stories on newspapers happening in other villages around South Africa.

It is a usual occurrence in villages and semi-urban areas in South Africa for female senior citizens who mostly stay alone or with small grandchildren to be attacked as they are soft targets. They bear the brunt of being labelled, accused, insulted, and isolated. An old person who is living alone, ugly, too dark, wrinkled, and has cracked feet (some of them)—these are the full evidence of witchcraft. After living a life of fear in their old age, they eventually die an excruciating death at the hands of young people.

Men and middle-aged women also fall prey to the spurious accusations but on a lesser extent. This heinous crime is being perpetrated by young people who should be instrumental in community-building initiatives and should be the ones who are open-minded and lead a crusade of destroying the myth instead of bolstering it through their disgusting actions, especially in rural areas that are inherently underdeveloped. But their energies are spent on negative issues rather than on positive progress. This is the same situation of belief crimes that have engulfed the world over, like terrorism.

The leaders of the countries affected by belief crimes are in constant denial about the causality of the crimes. They dubbed it pure evil, whereas the perpetrators of evil confirm the opposite. Almost all religious beliefs are implicated in terrorism. The main issue is reporting it depends on who is following the story or who first broke the story. Anybody who watches the news and reads newspapers both on print and online should be familiar with the religion that is associated with terrorism. Whenever people of that religion commit crimes anywhere around the world, that specific religion will be mentioned, but when a crime is committed by someone of other religions, it will just be about a man who shot dead two people. No religion name will be attached even if the perpetrator claims to be representing that particular religion.

In Scandinavia Norway in 2012, Anders Breivik, a Christian terrorist, a young farmer, and a right-wing white supremacist massacred more than fifty people because he was opposed to the Islamisation of Europe. Not surprisingly, he was not called a terrorist. The Islamic State in Syria and

Iraq is murdering people daily and not surprisingly, they are referred to as the world's richest terrorists.

We know that the majority of religious people are good. The number that carry out the attacks in the name of the beliefs is minimal, but the damage is substantial. Witch hunters commit crimes to fulfil their beliefs—that of chasing a never-ending war against evil. They practise their beliefs through physical attacks.

Witchcraft deeply embedded

The following words are from the famous South African political activist Steve Biko, who died in detention prior to democracy. I am not sure whether if he was still here, the same words will still be relevant to him, but I will quote him anyway.

We the black consciousness movement do not reject it witchcraft. We regard it as part of the mystery of our cultural heritage, whites are not superstitious, and they do not have witches and witch doctors we are the people who have this. Niehaus, 2001. 183

But Steve Biko, despite his utterances, would not have approved the murder of the so-called witches. When I was growing up, I did not know any evil that is present other than witches and their resultant deeds. I only came to understand Satan thereafter. In the African culture, there are no methods to guard against Satan, not even a single witch doctor and traditional healer have the purported know-how of driving out the mighty devil. The only precautions that were widely used were/are against witches.

My grandfather was a healer; he used to fortify our home and ourselves only against witchcraft, not Satan. He would fortify our home with a mixture of herbs (concoction) outside and inside the house. He would cut small openings in our flesh with a sharp razor blade to insert the herbs so that it mixed with our blood. That would be a complete fortification against any witch or witches together with their evil spirits, and thereafter, he would tell us that we must not be afraid nothing will touch us. Our home and ourselves—we are strong. This type of practice is ubiquitous in South Africa and the rest of Africa, I reckon.

According to our culture, when the boys reach the stage of maturity, they must go to the mountain (initiation school) to cast off boyhood and obtain manhood. It is the passage from being a boy to being a man, an age-old tradition; ceremonies and feasts are conducted.

Before I expand on this issue, let me make you aware that the yearly deaths of initiates in our province, the Eastern Cape, is due to the inexperience of moneymakers and chancers who practise circumcision without the guidance of the elders. The authorities are calling them illegal initiation schools. In some areas, this tradition has been abandoned a long time ago, but now the present generation is trying to revive it without any precedent. The province is very big, with different clans doing different traditions and customs. In our area, these types of events are very rare.

Back to my story. A traditional healer will be required to armour us against witchcraft and fortify all places that will play host to the festivities. Accordingly, this is a very sensitive stage where protection is of paramount importance. Since the young men were the future leaders, no risk is entertained. The traditional healers in our area are known for this job of protecting the initiates. They are designated due to their skills and experience, and no starters are allowed to gamble with the lives of the young men. That is the seriousness with which everyone regarded the risks posed by the evil spirits and spells. But risk from whom? The answer is telling; it is none other than witches, of course.

While I was still living with my grandparents at home, after school and during the weekends and school holidays, my duty was to look after the cattle as this was the norm, all the boys whose parents own livestock have to look after those animals. My younger brother was still young to go to the veld, and he would be playing with his contemporaries, while I was in the veld. One night my grandparents decided that it was not safe for my sibling to loiter around the village during the day. As a child, he was an easy prey to be bewitched; he would easily grab anything given by people and eat it. Witches might put a potion in the food, and he could fall sick and also come carrying that bad omen to the family house. In that manner, it was deemed that the whole family was vulnerable. So he should rather go with me to look after the cattle, and yes, he did go with me to the veld, and I carried a lunch box for him. This precautionary measure was against witches.

It is a norm for old and young people not to just accept anything or just eat anywhere. And if you think human beings are the only ones that are not safe, you are mistaken. You must think again. The non-talking creatures are also victims of this magic-frenzy, baboons or monkeys— those are the usual suspects—and cats and snakes to a lesser extent. But the animals are interchangeable; they can be of good use not by the witches but by the people who consulted the healers to strengthen or guard their riches, such as livestock, shops, etc. There are people who are successful in the villages in terms of owning innumerable sheeps, goats, etc., and they are not so lucky to be omitted either in the magic frenzy. They can be alleged of using a snake or a tortoise in increasing their stock.

There are also animals associated with witchcraft. Isak Niehaus called them the witches' familiars. For his book *Witchcraft, power and Politics,* Niehaus made an extensive research about witchcraft in the lowveld (Northern provinces of South Africa) areas. The Tsonga witches' familiars are believed to be nocturnal birds, hippopotami, crocodiles, or duikers. In my area, we were very fearful of an owl because it was a bird regarded as under the employ of witches. And there was also a legend in the village that during the night, there was a grotesque baboon walking the streets of our village, pulling a chain. This frightened us from walking during the nights. In all these, no mention of Satan was heard.

Witchcraft as an evil in our midst is deeply rooted. Our everyday language is littered with witchcraft-related swearing words. It is not uncommon to hear the words 'that witch, that witch' when there is an argument between people. One's enemy can be referred to as having a heart of a witch, meaning he/she is wicked and cruel. In South Africa there is a phrase or a sort of an idiom that is widely used during the traditional ceremonies, feasts, government events, or families coming together.

The praise singers would utter these words, and these are rarely omitted: 'Ukwanda kwaliwa ngumthakathi.' It literally means 'Prosperity and progress are only denied or blocked by the witch.' Even the people who do not really care about witches or witchcraft do utter these words. The meaning of these words is very deep and carries a heavy burden, especially to those that are persistently labelled as witches. I do not think by any means that it is easy to carry the burden of family and community misgivings caused by you as a person.

Now, magic continues on the road to riches. The ritual murders and killing of people are for creating a magic of luck and wealth through the body parts, especially for designated groups, such as children, twins, and albinos. By the way, the albinos are an endangered species in Tanzania. The witch doctors there regard the body parts of albinos as very effective in bringing luck and business success.

According to a UN report released in the year 2012, in South Africa an estimated three hundred lives are lost per year. Their tissues are ripped off while alive for nonsensical non-existent magic and spells. Most of the victims are children since the monsters think or believe that their tissues are more effective. In South Africa the number of children disappearing is alarming. The children are later found with decomposed bodies and with some body parts missing. The witch doctors employ people to go rip the body parts of the victims while they're still breathing, causing untold pain and suffering before death, as this will render the concoction its strength. It is said that the victim must scream to provide power to the concoction.

These correlate with what has always been narrated in general conversations flying around for a very long time that if the victim did not cry while a part is being ripped off from the body, the attackers will just abandon him/her because the tissue will not be effective or magical enough for use in the spells. There are unconfirmed reports of those who cheated this excruciating death by just staying or playing dumb when the attackers start to cut or stab their bodies. If the victim does not scream, it is said that the killers will just run away and not do anything since they will realise that it will be a waste of time to stab or cut a victim who does not scream. That would render that body part useless.

In some cultures in our country, when certain ceremonies are conducted, as usual a beast or sheep is sacrificed. If that animal does not make any noise before dying, this will be treated as a demonstration that all is not good it is a bad omen. If the opposite happens, it is a sign of good things to come. As I stated earlier, the **witch doctors pillar number 3** of witchcraft belief are part and parcel of the scourge because they have a lot to gain than to lose. Their very existence means a lot. They are not there to chase away the mighty devil. The core duties of witch doctors is to chase away the witches, not the devil. If the society can stop believing in the existence of witchcraft, our main and ultimate objective, their existence too is not guaranteed. They thrive on pinpointing innocent people, predicting lies and nonsense. These witch doctors (affectionately known in South Africa as *isangoma*) cannot even predict if rain will come the following day, but they can pinpoint innocent citizens as perpetrators of evil spells and dictate the death of somebody. These people have ravaged the nations through their lies. Family members are pitted against one another. Communities fight among themselves because of lies. It is very rare for witch doctors to confess that he/she cannot predict someone's fate or see through the problems of the sick. They would rather lie, taking money from desperate people and also taking advantage of their belief in magic.

Since witchcraft does not exist and is itself a lie, then the question might be asked, what is the armour of witchcraft protecting and from whom? It means they are protecting nothing from nothing. Their survival depends on lying and causing chaos in the community, ripping off the people's hard-earned cash that is desperately needed in these tough times of economic meltdown and recession. The belief in magic has dire consequences for any nation. It can be of organised religion or indigenous traditional belief; it does not make any difference. These beliefs themselves are not singing in one voice, they are enemies to one another. Some say others' belief is not true and vice versa. This is the modus operandi of Christianity in South Africa—to denounce and degrade the traditional African ancestral religion as backward, uncivilised, demonic, and standing against the word of God.

My other main goal in this book is to highlight the fact that Christianity was never and will never be better than ancestral religion. Both religions are in one bowl; they belong to the world of Harry Potter. This notion of one religion being better than the other is full of foolishness and ignorance. Then one must ask a question. If two fictions throw accusations and counter-accusations against each other about their real existence, which is neither here nor there for both of them, something serious must have gone wrong in our heads.

According to Niehaus, 2001 (185, 186), apartheid also played a role in the South African situation. By the segregation of the white minority regime, there was a land exclusively reserved for occupation by black

Africans, and this ostensibly ensured African self-government and African maintenance of institutions and culture. In the lowveld of South Africa, the state guaranteed chiefs' control over the land to deal with the native laws and customs. The chiefs were allowed to accede to the demands of the villagers in controlling witches. The chiefs tried cases involving witchcraft, mediated and also authorised witch diviners to determine the guilt of the accused, condoned the ritual humiliation of those identified as witches, and ensured that the bewitched were duly compensated in cattle for the crimes committed against them. Chiefs and their councillors also sought out and punished witches who stopped the rain. The chiefs did gain legitimacy by being seen as the protectors of the community from the harm of witchcraft evils and magical spells.

In my village, unlike the lowveld region, the chiefs do their job of mediating the conflict between the accusers and the accused, but they do not take part in giving diviners and witch hunters any power. If somebody consults a witch doctor to pinpoint or predict anything, that was regarded as a private matter between the individual and the family concerned. We grew up knowing that it is a closely guarded secret to consult a witch doctor or a traditional healer because that involves the health and the well-being of the whole family, their future plans, etc. That is why most of the time the witch doctor is consulted during the night. Alternatively, he/she may pay a visit to the concerned family during the night to fortify the family home and the rest of the family.

The reason behind the secrecy is to guard against counterattacks because if the enemies of the family or the witches can see who is being consulted, they will easily infiltrate the family. If they find out who is fortifying the family maybe they know his/her means of fortifying. This type of consultation is reminiscent of the modern doctor–patient relationships wherein the details of the patient are between him/her and the doctor. Usually, the family will consult a witch doctor that is far-flung just to avoid being seen by the people they are trying to guard against. Even if the results of the consultation are positive, people should be kept in the dark about what made the family to succeed or about the healing of a certain member of the family who was sick.

In these cases, the witch doctors are using magic for good reasons for the benefit of the society. In other words, they are practising white magic, working to heal, unlike the witches, who work during the nights, hurting people and using their magic in darkness—black magic. I do think that the witch doctors in the lowveld that Niehaus is referring to are those that were desperate for cash and fame because as a norm, a witch doctor is never consulted in public. Niehaus also explained that the chiefs also needed legitimacy, so they had to do what they needed to do—use witchcraft as a scapegoat to strengthen their kingdoms, authorising these diviners to pinpoint the so-called witches in public.

There is a vast difference between a healer and a witch doctor. I myself have previously consulted a witch doctor when I was a believer of the supernatural. I thought my fate and my things would be better, but lies will always be lies, and the reality did set in. I am very happy where I am today, believing in reality, not fiction.

Being a witch doctor is a calling from the ancestors of the family for a particular person who must obey this call of duty to work in the community. Some of his/her duties will be making predictions, healing the people, and protecting them from evil spirits or witches, of course. He/she will go to the initiation school until he/she finished the process under the guidance and tutelage of a senior witch doctor.

At the present moment in South Africa, this has got out of control. There are many witch doctor initiates all over the place because the belief or tradition like any other thing has graduated into a lucrative business venture. Any witch doctor now can do the job of initiating new recruits just to make some rand and cents. But to be fair, why should they be left out of money-making schemes while other religions are raking billions of rand from the masses? No wonder the witches will not stop flying in our heads.

The traditional healers or the herbalists are the equivalent of the modern doctor, who trains in the university for seven years. This was prevalent before the white men and women set foot on African soil. They were expert on coughs, fertility herbs, headaches, wounds, flu, and many more diseases, except for the sophisticated procedures, such as surgery and organ transplant. These healers cannot be put in one bowl with witch doctors. Yes, some witch doctors do the job of physical healing as the healers do, but being a traditional healer or herbalist is not child's play as some might think. It is carefully handed down from generation to generation. It is a painstaking job; it is researched and goes through trials, though not in laboratories.

African herbs help many people, including myself. Not all witch doctors are corrupt. There are those who are honest enough to surrender when the going gets tough. And not all traditional healers are unscrupulous; they have kept the nation alive for tens of thousands of years until today as I am writing this book.

The magic now is playing in the benches of the courts of law. The South African justice systems did not come to the rescue of the so-called witches who were under siege the conviction rate was minimal as expected. That shows that the problem is not treated with the urgency it deserves and is not regarded as serious. Between the period of 1985 to 1995, a total of 389 alleged witches were brutally killed, their homes destroyed, and their children were denied schooling in those areas. Between the same period mentioned above, the courts prosecuted only 109, 52 per cent of the 209 people accused of participating in witch killings; 12 were given wholly suspended sentences, 4 were sentenced to be whipped with a light cane, and 84 were imprisoned for periods varying from eighteen months to life imprisonment.

According to Niehaus, judges often treat the belief in witchcraft as an extenuating circumstance. I think the men and women of the bench, by acting in this manner, are further bolstering the non-existent myth by making it exist through their unfortunate actions. How can a qualified, learned judge reason with something that has not provided tangible evidence before him/her? Then how can we expect a layman to just forget or abandon the dreadful witchcraft belief? This is naturally impossible.

The drama of magic continues in the courts of law. In the case *state* vs *Mathabi*, the Honourable Justice Van der Walt considered sentencing to death four of the accused who have pleaded guilty of murder, but he accepted their claim that they had thought the deceased was a witch and reduced the penalty to a mere five years imprisonment, of which two years were suspended. Mind you, this is the modern South Africa, not medieval Europe. This is really sickening and unacceptable. People are allowed to gamble with other people's lives just as simple as that. As if this is not enough, here again the women and the men of the bench showed their consistence in recognising witchcraft as true.

It is said that judges recognised witchcraft as suitable grounds for appeal in a brutal murder case in the Bantustan reserve of Venda. A certain Mr Naledzani Netshiavha woke up after he heard a scratching sound on his door. Naledzani picked up an axe, went outside, and chopped down an animal hanging from the rafters of his roof! After it fell to the ground, he chopped it twice more. Villagers came to see the animal and described it as a donkey or a large bat but said that it later assumed the shape of an elderly man who was reputed as a witch. Naledzani had killed a man. A judge in the supreme court of Venda sentenced him ten years in prison for culpable homicide. As a norm, the sentence was subsequently reduced to four years on appeal in the Bloemfontein (Mangaung) appeals court. In 1991, 6 men who had stoned and burned to death 4 alleged witches were convicted of murder but were sentenced only 5 years' imprisonment, wholly suspended on condition that they underwent 100 hours of community service. Niehaus, 2001.

The above-mentioned ridiculous sentences of the perpetrators of violence against the imagined crime of witchcraft only serve to entrench the belief in witchcraft among the members of the South African society. These are some of the factors that are contributing to the validation of witchcraft belief, not its demise.

One afternoon, I was returning from the capital town of South Africa, Pretoria. It is now known as Tshwane, a disputed name that has caused some court challenges and protests by some members of the white communities in South Africa who feel that the city they have ruled for many years must not change its name. They contend that their culture and heritage are under threat and that there is a deliberate attempt to decimate them by this incumbent black majority regime in the name of transformation. Anyway, politics is politics.

I was researching for my book in the state library, the new state-of-the-art building. It was my first time visiting this new building. I never visited the old one either. While I was there, I developed some jealousy since I was staying far away from this magnificent storage of wisdom. I caught a midday train full of students bound for Johannesburg, and I was standing as the carriage was full to capacity mostly with students from vocational colleges. I was not bothered. I am used to this it is my favourite mode of public transport, but crowding that leads to pushing and shoving is not good.

When we were in the middle of the journey, halfway to Johannesburg and halfway from Pretoria, there came a man of God from another carriage, holding a holy book as a tradition. He greeted us all in the name of Jesus Christ. He belonged to the revivalist churches, and he told us that he used to preach in open sermons and tents. He quoted the verse that said to love everyone and trust no one. After preaching, he closed the sermon with a short prayer, after which he asked for some donations. Some donated with a variety of coins (R5,

R2, etc.) I would have liked to donate, but my coins were out of reach, and I was standing. I got no problem in donating a little amount that I can afford.

Then I asked the well-dressed pastor if he ever believed in the existence of witchcraft. As I was saying it in vernacular, he also responded in vernacular: 'Yes, there is witchcraft, and it is real. You must remember that we are in Africa. Even overseas, there is witchcraft. After all, where does the word *wizard* and *witches* emanate from?' These two words, *wizard* and *witches*, he uttered them in English. That was the end of our witchcraft chat—so sharp and brief. From there, my fellow riders asked him about money that is being made by the revivalist churches. The pastor responded by saying there is nothing wrong in donating huge amounts of money to the church. He boldly defended his position on money until we were separated in the Johannesburg train station.

Witchcraft belief victims forgotten

The ongoing anti-xenophobic campaigns are long overdue in South Africa. This scourge is taking us back to where we came from as humanity and (recently in South Africa) what humanity fought against for centuries, our superficial differences. I wish racism, sexism, homophobia and tribalism could have been included. They are interlinked. Their disgusting objective is to divide the human species.

The continuing killings, burnings, maimings, and displacement of the so-called witches and their families in South Africa do not in any case threaten the economy or the image of the country abroad. They do not discourage the much-needed investment that would contribute to the creation of the much-needed jobs; neither are they scaring away the all-important revenue generator that is tourism. The witchcraft murders do not make international headlines that will damage the brand of South Africa.

In view of the above-mentioned significant factors, there is not a chance that this scourge that seems to affect the not well-to-do who are staying in rural areas and the uneducated senior citizens could catch such attention—unlike the xenophobic attacks that occurred in April 2015. This is not the first time though, they occurred in 2008. The government denied that the cause of killing the African immigrants is due to xenophobia, they attributed the violence to rampant crime that is prevalent in South Africa. This time again there was no difference crime was blamed. The lips of the head of state and his cabinet were defending the indefensible. In other words, the victims of witch hunt died and suffered in silence in the new democratic South Africa, known all over the world for being in the forefront of human rights protection and for having world-renowned icons and internationally recognised struggle heroes and the most progressive constitution in the world.

The authorities do not see this as an emergency. In fact, this scourge is older than xenophobia. What we hear from them is just condemnation if a particular incident is fortunate enough to grace the airwaves. Since a considerable number of them go unnoticed (death in silence), it would be a daunting task to draw the necessary attention of the authorities without using the media. If the media is moving away from the issues of the society and the nation as a whole, a catastrophe is ahead of us. Due to historical reasons, our media is concentrated in the urban centres of our land.

I tend to think that the status of the victims plays a major role in drawing attention and urgency that is required of the state. As I move up, down, and around, engaging on my daily activities in the city that I reside in, Johannesburg, I see big advertising billboards written with 'Stop xenophobia.' I have not seen such an emphatic message regarding the killings of the so-called witches. Not that this is wrong; it is okay, but it must also be extended to the forgotten victims of witch-hunts.

Our state president even postponed the awarding of the national orders in Pretoria, which recognises the South Africans and foreigners who contributed to the development and advancement of South Africa and its people due to xenophobic violence. I wish this good gesture is also extended to the victims and families of witch-hunts. The provincial and local leadership should be deployed to go and dowse the fires happening now. Our media is inundated with adverts and slogans declaring that xenophobia is a crime against humanity. Rightly so, but they should consider witchcraft murders too. I urge the authorities and the community at large to show this vigour to the witch-hunt murders. If a campaign of this magnitude is possible, the campaigns to stop belief crimes might be a success too.

Witchcraft an excuse for non-success

Witchcraft is the perfect excuse for the lack of success for some people since this belief inculcates the idea that any failure in every sphere of society does not come naturally or is not due to neglect or laziness or any other social factor. Magic would be brought in in the form of an evil spirit, and obviously that evil spirit is not from space; its host is right in our midst. The places of learning do not enjoy any immunity either.

At school during examinations, there are allegations that some students are feeling drowsy due to a potion in the possession of a certain student who wants to pass the exams at the expense of other students. This potion's duty is to put some sort of veil over the eyes of other students.

It is even worse at workplaces since the jobs are scarce and getting hired is competitive in the face of high unemployment rate. Workplaces nowadays are the epicentre of competition. There are accusations upon accusations and counter-accusations of some employees using potions or magic acquired from their mothers, who are witches or diviners back home to gain an advantage. This is very irrational indeed. If one has magic or a magic potion, why bother looking for employment in the first place and be subjected to the rules and regulations laid down by somebody at work, leaving the comfort of your family and forfeiting your freedom?

That is the good thing about the beliefs. They want one to suspend his/her reasoning so that they strike hard. Even the witch doctors and the traditional healers and pastors are raking in thousands of rands in this magic frenzy by selling magic water, magic oil, and concoctions and/or offering even a simple prayer to the employees or prospective employees, so that they are favourable to the employers. To tell the honest truth, the above-mentioned revered members of the community are the ones who are not even smiling but laughing on their way to the bank to deposit and invest the free money coming from the magic-minded masses.

CHAPTER 2

Pillars of African witchcraft

Pillar no 1 African ancestral religion

Ancestral worship is very much alive and kicking in South Africa. My grandparents were practising what I called dual worship, worshipping the God of Abraham and the ancestors. It was easy because they are compatible to each other in many ways their convergence point is magic. I will discuss later the similarities of all beliefs. Wherever there is a need to consult, ask, or appease the ancestors, it is done through feasts and ceremonies. Our traditional sorghum beer has to be brewed to be used to communicate to the ancestors in front of the family elders and in some cases, villagers. Sometimes a goat or a sheep is slaughtered as part of the feast. The meat is dished up and served to the people according to the status of the members of the community—first to male elders and then to middle aged men and so on usually in the kraal, females elders dish up in the house according to seniority—the age-old tradition of African culture.

The kraal is the most sacred place and, in some instances, it ranks above or equal to churches in status to some families. It is used to conduct traditional ceremonies, to communicate and pray to the ancestors, to keep the livestock, an eating place for men even after a funeral. It is also the burial place for the head of the house, mainly a patriarch of the family. And more than anything, it is the sign of pride and authority of the male figures in many homes and families. God of Abraham have no place in the African kraals. This African sacred place is reserved for the African traditions.

Switching to the house of the Lord was never a steep slope to climb. My grandparents would go to church on Sundays, like folks in New York and Brazil. They were devout Methodists, fully participating on every activities of the house of the Lord. When there are problems, they would turn to both the God of Abraham and the ancestors for salvation.

The ancestors play a very important role in the lives of people who worship them. New developments within the family have to be communicated to them so that they can give their blessings and look after all that was brought to their attention. A newly built house must be reported to the ancestors so that it is under their guard, especially if it is outside the homestead. They need to be notified and be fetched from the old homestead to the new one. Even a car that is bought have to be reported. In opening a new home, it will depend on the family or a clan how they will carry out the ceremonies some would brew the traditional sorghum beer, slaughter a goat or a sheep, or both.

We are told that our ancestors are always with us wherever we go, looking after us. That is why if there is some misfortune in the family, it will be attributed to the wrath of the ancestors. It used to be said that since modernisation or Westernisation had made inroads in to traditional African culture, some elders, traditional leaders and healers, witch doctors, and the laymen on the street, attribute our misgivings to the abandonment of the traditional African culture and by grabbing the unsuitable white culture, which is not tailor-made for us. As a consequence of this deviation, our ancestors have given us their backs they are punishing us for leaving an age-old culture they themselves practised. This is a general rhetoric for some South Africans.

When my grandfather was laid to rest, both Christian and traditional African ceremonies were conducted in full force.

By the time the corpse arrived from the mortuary, a goat was placed at the doorway to welcome home the head of the family. The elders of the family welcomed him back to his house before laying him to rest the following afternoon. Thereafter, the goat was taken to the kraal to be slaughtered. In the house, the church took over the preaching, praying, and singing as is normally done. Few hours later, an ox was slaughtered in the kraal.

Traditionally, when the deceased is a male figure, an ox skin is presented to him as his blanket for eternal sleep, not physically but symbolically. The coffins are their eternal 'blanket' in these modern times. When the deceased is a female figure, a cow is sacrificed. Before the beast is killed, the elders would talk to the deceased. All these depend on the family or tribe or clan.

The funeral service from the morning up until the funeral procession to the graveyard in the afternoon (in our area funerals are conducted in the afternoon), the service was fully conducted by the church. The following morning, all the clothes of the deceased were taken by the older women of the village to the river to be cleansed before anyone can use or wear them. But this is no longer practised now. Four days after the funeral service, when the family mourning period was over, the traditional sorghum beer was brewed for this little ceremony.

Westernisation has gained ground in black society in South Africa, especially in rural areas, and surprisingly, there are those in rural areas who do not practise the entire African culture. If the time has arrived for their boys to shed off boyhood, they just take their boys to initiation school without slaughtering a beast and brewing the traditional beer in their ceremonies. Only cold drinks, bread and cakes are dished out. Some of those people claim to practise Christian lives.

Most of the people who have done away with the traditional African culture are mostly in urban centres. Those who still practise it are doing it partially. I think some of the reasons are city by-laws, since they were not designed to accommodate African cultural activities the zoning of areas, make it difficult to perform certain rituals in the absence of kraals, mountains, forests, and open velds for grazing of the livestock. The other significant factor is the fast pace of modernisation in the urban centres, which automatically render the indigenous cultural practices redundant.

Ancestral worship was the way of life in my home. I remember one evening during the 1980s. It was a winter month, as usual my two grandparents and I were sitting around the fireplace (called *iziko* in our Nguni language). Usually, it is located in the centre of the house. My granddad was a pipe smoker. Accidentally, the tobacco in his pipe just spilled to the floor. Before he lit the pipe again, he carefully collected the tobacco back to his pipe. The tobacco was spilled again for the second time. I don't know whether the pipe was facing downwards or sideways. That was when my granddad abandoned collecting the tobacco again. He said the ancestors needed to smoke and it was them who took down his tobacco. It was not an accident as he had thought when the tobacco spilled for the second time, that was when he realised that there was something not normal. He instructed my grandmother not to sweep it that same evening the forefathers must be left alone to smoke, so she must sweep it the following morning. Rightly so, my grandma swept it the following morning together with the ashes of the fire.

Though he is a man of God, my grandfather seemed not to have forgotten his roots, the traditional African religion in the form of ancestral worship. He had no problem in balancing the two to fit in his own life and his family. It was just normal. The same is true today in many African families who still practise this double worship.

Now I am asking myself a question. At the time when my granddad said to my grandma that she must not sweep the spilled tobacco and that she must rather sweep it the following morning, why did he say so? Probably my old man knew that by the following morning, it would still be lying there. In normal circumstances, if the tobacco is smoked, it should be finished or turned into ashes as what would happen when he puffed his pipe. But that was not the case. Perhaps my granddad was doing what he was supposed to do the way he was told or the way he grew up experiencing the same situation.

This question I am asking now, I did not ask it the moment this took place. I was young and knew nothing about religion. What was happening to me was that I was just watching and following the instructions. But now I know, I am able to separate truth from lies, facts from fables. It is just that I vividly remember those good old days staying with my grandparents and now, I am in a fortunate situation to compare and analyse.

The same situation that I have just narrated is no different from the culture that is being practised by millions in my homeland. It is regarded that the ancestors are not really dead in the true sense of the word. Ceremonies and feasts are held to give food to the ancestors as a way of gratitude for a prosperous life and general well-being. Somebody can ask for a leave from his/her workplace, especially from big cities like Johannesburg and Cape Town, just to pay a visit to their homes to give the ancestors food. Goat and sheep will be sacrificed, and the traditional sorghum beer is brewed. Family members and fellow villagers are invited. All the food and the traditional beer will be consumed by the living.

People feel indebted to the ancestors they cannot just live a secular life. If the living do not obey the laws of the clan, family, and nation as a whole, the wrath of the ancestors will befall them. There will be natural disasters, civil strife, and bad luck to the individuals and all these misgivings that will be attributed to disobedience to the ancestors. The people will be required to appease the ancestors and go back to practising the culture and tradition as per the ancestors' requirements.

Similarly, in the organised written religion if one does not go to church, pray, obey all the rules of the church, and follow the Ten Commandments they feel guilty and repent and ask for mercy from the Almighty God. Some intellectuals say Africans do not pray to the ancestors they only venerate them. But as an open-minded person, I don't rely on what somebody says to me. I don't see any difference in praying to god and in praying to the ancestors. The way and the manner in which Africans pray to the god of Abraham is no different to what they do for the ancestors. However, when the same practices that are practised when praying to the god of Abraham are practised when praying to the ancestors, this is not regarded as prayers the apologetics say no, we just venerate them. It is crystal clear that there is no difference here, perhaps some Africans feel embarrassed being seen as praying to the dead in the eyes of the western religion, sometimes not realising the similarities or core foundations of the above-mentioned religions which is non-existent magic.

In both instances, there are laws to be observed. The holy Bible has got Ten Commandments that need obedience and observance otherwise, the Almighty will unleash his wrath in many ways. In other words, God will punish those who deviate from his laid-down laws. From Genesis to Revelation, the holy book is full of the methods of punishments that will be meted out, ranging from stoning to death to causing plagues. The same applies to the traditional African ancestral religion. If the community or societal rituals, customs, and traditions are abandoned and/or ignored, the ancestors will unleash their wrath by inflicting pain and suffering through natural disasters, infertility, etc.

As I said earlier the ancestors like God are deeply admired and respected. According to the editors of the *Encyclopaedia of African Religion 1* Asante and Mazama 2009: 47 the ancestors are in a spiritual state of existence that gives them the power to assist those who are living (the same as god, who is regarded as living in spirit). People have believed for a long time that the ritualised propitiation and invocation of ancestors can influence the fate of the living. My main argument here is that I don't understand when the two editors in page 51 Enclopedia of African religion 1, 2009 said, 'People do not pray to the ancestors they rather pray to god, but they ask for intercession.' They went on to say, 'No Africans pray to their ancestors any more than they pray to their living fathers the prayer is reserved for the gods.'

Maybe it is the way they see it, but practically it is not the case. Why do I say that? It is because of the similarities between praying to god and to the ancestors, which I have already mentioned above. Some African intellectuals and ordinary people even use words like *intermediaries (meaning the ancestors act between the living and god or they are the messengers of people to god because they are nearer to god) when referring to the ancestors because of the fear of being labelled ungodly and primitive. I don't know when the time will arrive for the Africans to stop always apologising for nothing.* Where I come from, there is a time for praying to the God of Abraham in the presence of the holy book and a time for praying to the ancestors in the presence of home-brewed sorghum beer and/or sacrificed goat (sometimes just plain and without anything in front of them when praying to the ancestors).

Just note the following sentences and see the total contradiction and how Asante and Mazama missed the point: (None of this process the process of worshipping and praying to ancestors) is a matter of good and evil, it is a matter of holding back chaos in the world. In fact the ancestors neither persecute their descendants nor punish for their wickedness, nor reward for the goodness. However the ancestors may harass or trouble the descendants for failing to religious submission or service. The ancestor is not a punishing authority, but a judge who is concerned with the prosperity of the lineage.'

Responding to these apparent contradictions, I say the ancestors are the punishing and rewarding authority like the god of Abraham because if the laws/ rituals of the clan, family, nation and tribe are observed, the ancestors will reward the society with fortunes, good health, rain, good harvest, healthy livestock etc. the family even sacrifice the animals invite family and friends just to say thanks to the ancestors for the success of the family or the clan, meaning the success is attributed to the ancestors in this case they rewarded the family for obeying all rituals, this happened in my home and is happening in many homes. but if the opposite happens, the bad will befall the society. The same is true to the Christian god obedience results in rewards, and disobedience results in punishments. Let me be pragmatic. Currently, in South Africa we are faced with many social ills and misfortunes. Many believers of ancestors are attributing these to the modern life that has annihilated the African culture. They commented that the forefathers are punishing us for embracing the white culture at the expense of the age-old indigenous African culture and religion.

In addition, the recent natural disasters in Asia the tsunami and hurricane Katrina in the United States of America that unfortunately took many lives are attributed to the disobedience of the laws of God. The pious are unequivocal in saying that god is punishing the sinners, that he is angry about abortion and homosexuality.

Speaking of god, let me list the two types of deities that are in play here. First is the African god. Before the arrival of the god of Abraham, Africans believed in and knew of a god as the creator of all things, but that god did not occupy the centre stage. He was/is impotent and inferior to the ancestors. Things were made worse by the arrival of the Christian god. By all indications this inferior African god never had any chance of dominating the lives of the Africans, however the ancestors were.

At the moment, when one talks of a god one talks about the God of Abraham, who is dominating and is in the process of uprooting ancestral worship, which sometimes is not in competition with him but supplements him as I explained. The ancestors in African religion have more weight than the impotent African god (before colonisation brought god of the desert). Ancestors were/are not venerated, but they were/are fully worshipped. When the Europeans set foot on African soil, they said the Africans did not know god. Presumably, they were referring to the god of Abraham, not the African god. They did not know the African god or did not understand him because he was on the backstage, enjoying inferiority to the ancestors. The centre stage or the front stage was/is always taken and occupied by the ancestors. Now that the African god has been permanently displaced by the desert god, he/she will forever rest in peace.

In turn, the god of Abraham is not safe or guaranteed a spot either. Science is approaching roaring with evidence, and reason is slowly waking up to take its rightful place in the world. That would ultimately cancel out the name *God* from the face of the planet, and anything related to god will end up in museums and libraries to be displayed for the future myth-free generations. We have seen how the African religion is still relevant in many communities in South Africa.

To connect this story with the theme of the book, as the things are in this manner, Satan is out of equation here. For people who are sticking to the African religion, to them the representation of evil is witchcraft. Whenever they pray to ancestors for evil protection, that would commonly be against the witches. It is unthinkable that the witchcraft belief will be cast out, while the religion that is portrayed as the armour against it or as its antidote (representing good) is left to exist.

Even if people do not kill the so-called witches, they will always believe that witchcraft exists. After all, who is evil when the ancestors are good? In this way, it is the pillar that keeps witchcraft belief alive and kicking with its brutal consequences of murdering senior citizens. Both of them must go. The only solution to this conundrum is to secularise the society. The following chapter is about another pillar of witchcraft belief—the churches.

Pillar no 2 the churches

The beliefs of the church have a big role in the persecutions of the so-called witches. This verse confirms this: 'You shall not permit a sorceress to live.' This verse is one of the myriad verses that gives the church authorities basis to pursue the witches through trials and executions, which prevailed in Europe from the late Middle Ages to the eighteenth century. These were also prevalent before the Middle Ages.

There are differences between Europe and Africa when it comes to witchcraft. In Europe, it is in libraries and museums, but it is a shock to many that it sporadically exists through African immigrants residing there. They crossed the high seas with the magic scourge in their heads. Back in the African continent, the compatibility of the Western religion and traditional African religion is very apparent.

Jean la Fontaine seems to know better about this magic problem. On March 1 2012, she meticulously laid out the indigenisation of Christianity on her writing in *The Guardian online*:

> In their present form beliefs in witchcraft is not 'traditional'—changes since earlier times are obvious. Modern beliefs see the power of witchcraft as emanating from the evil spirits that possesses the witch and endow him/her with the power to harm. This belief in possession by evil spirit has been promulgated in Africa by the western missionaries of the fundamental, particularly Pentecostal

Christian beliefs. It has enabled the Africans to retain a modified version of their former beliefs in witchcraft, obtaining the approval of Satan-hunting Christians whose life is dedicated to the pursuit of evil.

She commented on the gruesome killing of a Ghanaian teenager by the members of his family after being accused of witchcraft. According to the UN (United Nations) report: 2012, Churches especially those belonging to the Pentecostal and the prophetic movement (charismatic churches), plays an important role in the diffusion and legitimatisation of fears related to witchcraft, especially child witches.

The pastor-prophet figure is important in the process by effectively validating the presence of witchcraft spirit, and they actively participate in the fight against the evil of witchcraft. The report went further by stressing that the phenomenon is less significant in Islamic countries despite the lack of precise and detailed information. It has been said that since the 1980s, there has been a rise of various religious movements in the sub-Saharan Africa.

Pentecostalism is a religious movement in which followers claim personal experience with a supernatural force—the Holy Spirit. They believe that everyone can be saved by having faith in Jesus. The main purposes of these churches focus on their ability to use the presence of the Holy Spirit to fight against the satanic world that is incarnated by the witches, evil spirits, and ancestral spirits.

The personification of the demon in the figure of the witches enables the churches to declare war against Satan. These churches claim to cure incurable diseases, such as AIDS and cancer, putting the lives of their clientele in danger just because of money rush. The role of the pastor-prophet in the churches seems to be of major importance in their anti-witch-hunt campaign and their ability to identify the witches.

As recently as this year, a South African newspaper called *The Sowetan* (Wednesday 20 May 2015) ran a front-page story of a pastor confessing to be a witch and fully practising witchcraft. A priest's confession that he dabbles in witchcraft has led to an outbreak of violence. On Tuesday 19 may 2015, police fired rubber bullets and tear gas to diffuse the crowd of residents who set fire to the house of the priest in the township of Nancefield near the border town of Musina in Limpopo Province. The attack came after the Methodist Church priest admitted on a public satellite TV channel owned by the charismatic church that he practises witchcraft.

The newspaper confirmed to have seen the video where the pastor confesses. He explained that a certain spirit comes to visit him at a certain time. His wife would think that he is present, but his spirit is not there he goes to visit people's houses. He said he even taught his daughter so that if he is gone, the daughter will carry on the job. But the charismatic pastor (the witch pastor was confessing to) warn people not to kill anybody because of a confession unless god allows that. The police also confirmed the incident and said they had established a task team to tackle a growing spate of ritual killings and witchcraft-related violence that gripped some parts of the province.

This sort of story is not only confined to this province it is all over South Africa and Africa. Churches in South Africa command a considerable number of people. It would be a mammoth task and almost impossible to just expect an abrupt stop to the witchcraft myth. Not all revivalist churches thrive on the deliverance of witches. That also applies to the witch doctors not all of them participate in witch smelling.

I personally know of churches that do not even utter a word about witchcraft. When referring to the evil spirits and darkness, they stick to their traditional established Christian representation of evil, which is Satan. Why the churches have outlived their relevance? The answer is very simple they have adapted or evolved, the following sections on ideology, hope and profit present an answer to this question.

Church as a profit-making entity

The main drawcard of the Pentecostal churches is the promise of miracles and prosperity. I think it is their source of strength, and that will keep them in the business for a very long time. As long as humans are still magic minded, these churches are immune to the economic dynamics of the world. Many industries have closed down some are swallowed by their rivals. But this particular entity is not going to be a victim of those economic dynamics. Their clientele do not care whether they're living below or above the poverty line, they are going to donate anyway to oil and keep the spiritual wheels rotating.

Since secularisation is moving at a snail's pace. As time moves on, innovation seems necessary for any business to survive. This is a fast-paced, ever-changing globe and so is the house of God. Churches have to adapt or die a natural death, as the business experts say. That was the reason for the birth of the revivalist charismatic churches—to close the gap that the traditional churches could not close. They cater for the needs of their believers who are not prepared to be left behind by the ever-changing world. Their clever strategy is preaching, promising, and teaching what their followers want to hear or at least expect from them.

Considering this world of ours is riddled with chronic problems, from grinding poverty to unsuccessful love lives, who does not want to escape from these unwanted things? The revivalists are here to fulfil this duty or call. They thrive through false promises of fortunes, good health, miracle treatments, or solutions for anything under the sun that makes humans uncomfortable. Of course, those miracle promises do not come cheap or free. They are not running charities, they are here to make rand and cents.

There is a price to pay, or I can even say a higher price to pay—from donating your TV sets to giving away your own roof you and your family live under, one's hard-earned savings and cash, or your lifelong pension fund. The Word of God does not come cheap anyway because God will give back twice what you have given away in his name. The believers come in droves to witness the so-called (staged) miracles. The leaders of these churches will not abandon this commercial venture of making millions (which are not taxable) out of absolutely nothing.

My point is, how can we expect this to cease if it is a livelihood and business?

The belief system has evolved, and some of the religions have turned into businesses, especially those that are commercial ventures. They have caught the spotlight from the believers and non-believers. The rest of the so- called traditional churches, such as Anglicans, Methodist, Dutch reformed churches have been dwarfed by this spotlight—except for the Roman Catholic Church, which operates as a state or government in its city of power, the Vatican. It is the only traditional church that is still commanding media coverage and growth in the developing world.

The revivalist churches have become conglomerates. They operate their own media through their paid satellite channels. There they showcase twenty-four hours the benefit of being in their midst. These are manned by the highly regarded televangelists, who are more business minded than spiritual minded. For us secularists, this is a steep slope to climb because we are no longer dealing with old myth and irrational books. They have turned into a more complicated issue—business.

How easy it would be to secularise the world if some people had made businesses and livelihood out of false ancient ideas. It would have been very simple if we can just say, Please just close that book. Ignore it, it's not worth it. That would be a simple mistake. That book is worth a lot more than we can fathom.

Church as a giver of hope

Churches or organised religions play a pivotal role in unifying the community. The greatest advantage of belief is that it gives hope to the masses. Hope is a lifeline because it keeps us alive to realise our tomorrow. It keeps us alive to fulfil our dreams for the future or near future. Without clinging to hope, I do not see any one of us surviving until tomorrow to make the world a better place to live in. In the context of what is transpiring in the world, the word *hope* is synonymous to the word *life*. In the absence of hope, members of our species have unfortunately perished through their own hands in what educated people call suicide.

I suspect those fellow humans had hope vanished from their system. What else could have pushed them to reach those dreadful limits? I say dreadful limits because there are people who are terminally ill, in the vegetative state, mentally and physically incapacitated, and bedridden. Some of the above-mentioned people do wish a dignified death euthanasia, but it is illegal in many countries, including South Africa and it is legal in Netherlands. The number of suicides and the number of those terminally ill who wish for euthanasia are negligible compared to rest of the overall population. This means that many people do want to cling to life irrespective of their circumstances. In other words, this fire of hope is still burning inside their hearts.

I myself I am still alive due to the fire of hope that is still burning inside me. The father of the nation, the late Tata Nelson Mandela, had many quotes reflecting his faith in hope which have surprisingly turned into verses. Even his long stay in jail was inspired by nothing else but hope for justice. His quotes are used by both rogue and smart politicians, they all sing in one voice when they quote Madiba's words.

His famous quote 'It seemed impossible until it is done' resonates with many people, including myself. This strengthens humans to rise after each fall and to never give up. Considering what happened in the past to all humanity, it can be said that hope played a crucial part in keeping us up until today and hopefully through the coming generations. Where does the strength of hope emanate from? I know it is from inside, but what are the other factors outside our bodies that bolsters hope?

That will depend on your environment of upbringing or your general environment. If one's environment is a religious one, it will be an obvious case of where you get the strength of hope. If not religious, the explanation of hope will differ vastly. So far, many people are sticking to beliefs because they give them hope.

Why will I bother myself or inconvenience myself with some costs involved or slaughtering a goat to appease the ancestors if I do not hope for something or hope to achieve that something? Why will I fight tooth and nail to keep my church building from demolition if I do not have hope that if I enter the cathedral, I will obtain something that I have hoped for?

The holy texts of religions have got numerous verses giving hope. They not only giving hope for this life, they go further than that. They give a hope for life beyond the grave. Whether that hope will be fulfilled or realised, that is another issue. Can this be the answer to why the pious masses are clinging to their beliefs? Maybe some are not even interested whether the religions are right or wrong about the origins of life. The message of hope just revives them in keeping on pursuing life and their dreams.

In my own opinion, hope plays a pivotal role here. We go to school with the hope of better lives for ourselves and our families. We vote for a political party with the hope of better lives for us and our children. If an incumbent political party is dashing our hopes, it is removed with a ballot by some of us who are lucky to exercise that choice.

What about the people who do not entertain any of the beliefs that give hope (myself included)? Where do they get it? What keeps them going without relying on any institution that will instil hope? To be honest, hope is natural. I myself got high hopes like anybody who is worshipping. Possibly I have even got higher hopes than the pious masses. I do not have to rely on something to hope for something there is a fire of hope that is burning inside.

Then what is the difference between those who rely on something and those who do not look upon anything for hope but themselves? The beliefs are just receiving free credit, to be precise. What would be the alternatives for the masses if the beliefs are abandoned? Who will give them hopes? They need not worry. They can remain hopeful in spite of the lack of beliefs, like some us who got high hopes without relying on anything.

Religion as an ideology

Religion survives because it is an idea. Religion and politics do correlate as ideas. They are not far-fetched as some would think. In the past, much of the northern hemisphere was under the dictatorship of the pulpit. Today much of the Middle

East is under the dictum of the holy text. I sometimes always overhear some people, most of them followers of religion, saying religion does not mix with politics. They are a bit mistaken.

Religion has its own ideas on how the society must be structured and advances a vision of what should be done. This alone qualifies them to be an ideology. Their doctrine is clear and visible, and they preach those ideas on every sermon. Their ideas too are not immune to challenges. In other words, their ideas are in competition with other ideas, such as liberalism, communism, nationalism, and so forth. In much of the Western world and Africa, religion is not in control of the states, but it has a colossal influence that is leaning to theocracy in some states.

In the Middle East, where religion is in control of the states' resources and the entire populace, its existence is more than guaranteed, and it is the archenemy of liberalism. It has no threat in the form of opposition. The threat is on their side—the extremists, who want to rule by literally applying the holy text as it is, not omitting some verses that are considered too extreme or outdated by the ruling theocracies. As a matter of fact, ideologies replace one another through popular votes. But why is religion still surviving and relevant to the masses? It survives in spite of not being in government in the Western world and Africa because its ideas need to be incorporated in society.

And it has evolved. It is deeply involved in day-to-day community issues. That is how it keeps its relevance. Like a political party that received a crushing defeat in the polls, it does not lie down and go into extinction, it will regroup and fight back for its own survival and for what it stands for its values, vision, etc. It will keep the incumbent regime under close watch. So religion does not take things lying down either.

In fact, there are many religious Christian political parties in Europe and Africa. In South Africa, there are some represented in the national assembly. By feeding the hungry, fighting for those evicted, accommodating refugees, schooling the indigents, it makes itself relevant to the eyes of the believers and non-believers. Can the victims of evictions forget about the goodwill and mercy of God or religion? No. Even non-believers, as I said, would commend the work of religion in uplifting the community through its pragmatic approach to social problems.

Since help from religion may be received as goodwill or grace of God, religion as an ideology is kept relevant to the pious whether its doctrines are right or wrong as an ideology, so far it is safe. What about secular help? Can people be assisted outside the boundaries of the Holy Spirit? The answer is a resounding yes! Compassion and wickedness are human traits that are in our genes, while religion, tribalism, racism, homophobia, and sexism are learned.

All of us, pious and non-pious, we care and feel for one another irrespective of our ideologies, colour, or language. We even extend this compassion to other living beings, such as animals. There is a tendency to regard religious people as good or doing good things and non-religious people as doing the opposite this is a fallacy. As I said, both groups are capable of committing heinous crimes and are also capable of care and love.

Nature is greater and smarter than any religion that ever surfaced on this planet. To attest to this fact, which does not need any proof whatsoever, please read on carefully. The Abrahamic holy books are full of compassionate words and words of wisdom such as, to forgive, to love your neighbour, to not commit adultery. And in the same process, they contain horrific and terrible words that instruct humans to stone other humans to death and to enslave other human beings. This is a direct and clear evidence and signs that show nature overrides religion.

The desert tribesmen who jotted down and edited the holy text were not immune to the natural traits of compassion and wickedness. In my opinion, the horrific instructions in the holy books were made to scare people into bowing down to the irrational teachings. It goes without saying that the designers of the religions knew that some people would not accept and agree with the frivolous claims and inaccurate presentation of life on earth. The only solution was to suppress the dissent and instil permanent fear. They succeeded then, but not now.

All the ancient religions that are practised in the West and Africa have more similarities than differences. I mentioned this because they are the ones that are influencing our lives. They are Islam, Christianity, Judaism, traditional African ancestral religion and witchdoctors.

Here are their similarities;

1. They have survived for a long time.
2. They make unfounded and unsubstantiated claims about the origin of the universe and life.
3. Their doctrines insult reason.
4. They were founded when the ancient men had no alternatives available to explain the origin of life, the only explanation was supernatural.
5. They are going to survive for some time if the Enlightenment Project is stagnant as it is now.
6. They cause unnecessary loss of life—in the past, present, and probably in the foreseeable future.
7. Their claims cannot be proven in a court of law and stand the test in the laboratory.

8. They have plenty of followers that is not going to change any time soon. In the developing countries, the increasing trend is alarming. While in the developed countries, especially in the West, the trend is reversing, except in the United States of America.

9. The unstoppable science is relentless in its progress to lay waste to their ungrounded claims.

10. They all believe in the supernatural.

11. They are all given unfettered respect by the authorities, and their practice is guaranteed in the constitution.

12. They claim monopoly on truth and are sensitive to challenges.

13. All of them are homophobic.

14. Only secular values and science will dislodge them from their stranglehold on the masses of the world.

15. They thrive on the ignorance of the masses.

16. They have the propensity to instil permanent fear on the masses in order to apply conformity and entrench their dogmas.

Pillar no 4 the media

One of the enlightened sections of our society, the media in South Africa, which is the product of civilisation and is now enjoying the fruits of liberalism it also helped to establish, is reversing these gains. The media is the success of the Enlightenment Project. One would wish it to remain so to keep the enlightenment torch forever bright. The free media is very crucial in keeping an eye on democracy and human rights.

The media today is part and parcel of our lives. I don't know where we would be today without the media's watchful eyes in South Africa and Africa. Nowadays, it has grown in leaps and bounds, taking advantage of the twenty-first century's technological boom and innovation that is good news for all of us.

What do I mean by saying the media is reversing the gains of civilisation? The media is widespread as it is, it reaches the darkest corners of South Africa. Many people are exposed to the media (print, electronic, online, etc.) The media in South Africa has allowed itself to bow down to supernatural lies and frivolous claims by advertising false claims of miracle treatment for any disease, magic cures, and quick fixes to personal problems, fortune or money, promotion at work, etc.

The media knows very well that AIDS is incurable, but they advertise the messages claiming to cure it. In addition, the media fraternity knows that nobody can cure every disease or solve every problem under the sun in an instant or, worse of all, by not following the conventional means. All the impossible tasks that conventional means cannot achieve are being presented as just small fish to fry through false advertisements by the media of South Africa.

These supernatural claims by the bogus prophets and doctors with often-bizarre pseudonyms exacerbate the problems of supernatural belief. That is detrimental to our society, and in addition, they validate the unproven claims of beliefs that have engulfed our nation and the whole world. If we see an advert about a potion that claims to cure bewitched people and chase away the evil spirits, which from our community's perspective evil spirits emanates from witchcraft, what idea is being given to us? It essentially means this thing of witchcraft does exist and that it is true. This automatically strengthens our resolve and our world view about witchcraft.

In our community, when you talk of evil spells and spirits, there is nothing other than wizards, witches, and witchcraft. Now when you advertise an antidote for this malice, you have confirmed the existence of witches in our midst. To some, you have cast away any doubts, if there was any, about witchcraft, therefore inculcating and instilling what we do not need in this day in age (i.e. belief without hard evidence).

When a reputable daily or weekly newspaper that we trust and have been loyal to for many years show these non-existent dark claims, how difficult or easy not to believe them? Most of the time, the content of the newspaper is viewed as credible—editors' comments, sports columns, special editions, supermarkets' adverts, real estate's auction adverts, funeral notices, and so on. The objective of the above-mentioned items listed is to persuade the consumers to buy these products and use them.

The witchcraft antidotes also appeal to the consumers to buy them. Here is a taste of what I am talking about. This advert appeared on the *Sunday World* newspaper dated 10 May 2015 in the classifieds section.

Mind you, this paper is popular with the community, its background is defined by the belief in the existence of witches, black Africans, to be exact.

> DR JIM & MAMA FAITH! stop suffering we help & make your life a success in many services mainly, remove curse and bad spells, remove witchcraft and black magic infertility in woman and men, work, business, marriage problems, court cases, protection from enemies and many more, you come out of problems 100% guaranteed with permanent results and no side effects.

The contact details of the so-called doctor were listed at the bottom of the advertisement. So are the validations of the imaginary witchcraft belief that led to the brutal death of innocent senior citizens and the stigma attached to it.

These newspapers are manned by elite educated professionals, journalists, and newspaper companies that are controlled by learned managers and owners; all of them should know better and act better than this. Interestingly, the same newspapers who advertise this nonsense are the first to put a gruesome headline story, like that of a granny hacked and burned to death together with her grandchildren due to being accused of witchcraft. The same newspaper boldly advertised in the classifieds section at the back, a magic oil and herb that can cast away evil spirits of witchcraft and cure the bewitched and the possessed.

Then where do we stand? Why is the media of South Africa perpetuating a dark myth by advertising loads of nonsense? I do not in any case attribute the witchcraft and ritual murders to the media adverts. My point is, the advertisements validate the non-existent myth of witchcraft, and the belief itself fuels the unnecessary murders.

There is a certain best-selling daily newspaper in South Africa called the *Daily Sun*; it is in love with magic stories. Stories of zombies, *tokoloshes* are not rare to find in this particular paper. They just take the stories from the people and spread them as if they are true. This has lent credence to the myth. Unfortunately, this newspaper is most popular with the community whose lives are characterised by so much belief in and worship of God and ancestral spirits. The *Daily Sun* is continually feeding South Africans with out-of-mind gibberish almost on a daily basis. As a consequence, people love this magic newspaper because it is acting in their best interests by showing stories they need and expect.

All these magic stories of the *Daily Sun* have no evidence to support their narration. I mean, nobody was seen flying on top of a broom or using children to fly. The *Daily Sun* is making money out of these fictions they put on their front pages. They know that most South Africans are magic minded and are easily attracted by the stories of the so-called witches being caught red-handed.

On March 30 2015, the *Daily Sun* did it again, attracting throngs of myth believers by putting on the front page a clear coloured image of a naked black woman. The woman was sitting down, her hands tied with the rope that she claimed to be her transport to fly. Please read this story carefully and see how South Africa is made into a nation of jokers. Even believers would be dismayed by this.

A Flying Visitor Drops in on Pastor

The pastor could not believe his eyes when he saw a woman inside his locked house. She was naked sitting quietly on the floor. Her shit was in a bucket. The woman said she was flying on a rope when she fell into the pastor's house. The woman who said she comes from

Ebatsakatsini ['a place for witches' in the Swazi language] near komatipoort in Mpumalanga province, Nkomazi region identified herself only by her surname Mahlalela. She was caught in the home of Pastor Simon Singwane of the Back to the Word of God Church in Mbangwane village. The village of ebatsakatsini is the place created for the people evicted from any of the 54 villages around Nkomazi after being accused of witchcraft. Mahlalela [the caught woman] said they are a team and they work for one master. They were about fifteen holding on to the rope when they took off. We use a rope when we fly said a woman, and I was sitting at the back when I fell off, when the police arrived she told the officer that she was here to perform evil deeds on the family, but she was caught.

It is very disheartening that the majority of South Africans are thirsty for these types of stories about non-existent magic of all things. The media has the moral responsibility of not misleading South Africans but informing them with accurate news, reliable and honest advertisements.

The South African media is famously known for exposing dishonest politicians, which is commendable, especially when the public purse is being depleted for the wrong reasons. But they themselves should practise what they preach by refraining from advertising dishonest messages and showing on their front pages out-of-the-mind nonsense. Maybe they are doing this for money, but it is not worth it. They must stop exploiting the credulity of the masses. Taking the people back to the caves by glorifying ancient myths through advertisements of solutions based on magic and by writing imagined stories as facts does not bode well for the Enlightenment Project.

CHAPTER 3

Alternatives to dangerous myth

Ubuntu

If there is one thing that is missing today in the world, that thing is hidden within us as people. It has been evading us for a very long time. It is something that needs no volumes of books, no doctrines, no mysticism. It has the potential to alleviate the human species from the quagmire we find ourselves in today. If it was fully practised a long time ago by our forebears, we would not be in this situation today. We would not have had slavery, intertribal strife, civil wars, world wars, or anything that seem to degrade and destroy life or inflict pain, both emotionally and physically.

Today we have built billions of rand's worth of military hardware. These equipments were not invented to make food or medicine the goal is to kill and maim other living beings. The past wars have proven that. New technology was accelerated just to meet these unwanted demands, just for spurious reasons of dominating the world and eliminating those who do not look the same as others. At this moment in time, there are probably countries in the world who got more battle tanks than tractors used to plough the earth to produce the giver of life, which is food. As human species, we need innumerable spades than AK-47s. The task of the Kalashnikovs is not to till soil to plant the seeds of wheat, it is to cancel individuals from the face of the earth.

Of all the holy books that control the spirit of the people of the West and Africa, none of their tenets are founded on this substitute I am proposing. It has no chosen people, no apostasy, no commandments, no revelations, no authority, no claim on anything. The Africans had made a serious mistake by abandoning it. It was partly lived or is partly lived most of the time it survives as a concept that is abstract, not practical as it should be.

Instead, we opted for the unproductive and unnecessary path of engaging in worshipping invisible spirits and beings. We discarded what was supposed to be our own religion, if there is to be something called religion. Even the invading Abrahamic faiths missed the point, they should have adopted or copied this life-giving phenomenon and threw away their holy books that divided the human species into slaves, infidels, Gentiles, and non-Gentiles.

As you read these lines, I think you should have figured out what I am talking about. Ubuntu—this word says it all, nothing more, nothing less. If there is a god who is worthy of being worshipped, there is no need to go further than this. What fascinates me more about ubuntu is its rationality; it is based on human reasoning in its simplest form—common sense, neither complicated nor sophisticated. Just to think for others.

Its direct translation from the Nguni language is 'humanity'. As I said earlier, ubuntu does not discriminate on any basis it does not have tribes or denominations. Ubuntu does not have boundaries both in the mind and physically no questions are asked if one needs help. Many people in rural areas and other non-rural areas will exist as one and will unite in the face of grinding poverty. Nobody is killed because the society is poor. People share what little they have. What is holding them together it is ubuntu.

In South Africa there are many relief organisations and people that practise

Ubuntu, they are countless from soup kitchens to international relief organisations such as Gift of the Givers. Ubuntu is universal in the United States and elsewhere, the people are touched by the plight of the peoples of the so-called developing countries. The people of the United States and Europe, through their relief organisations, practise ubuntu in the real sense by flying to Africa and elsewhere to help their fellow species in need. Organisations such as USAID (United States Agency for International development), Oxfam, Red Cross, Doctors without Borders, and many others are founded on ubuntu. Ubuntu's mantra is 'Umuntu ngumuntu ngabantu'. You are what you are because of others.

It implies that without other human beings, nothing is achievable or possible. That is why, most of the time, I do not agree with this mantra 'everything is possible with god'. If that was the case, all of us should be living in harmony. This clearly shows that not everything is possible with god and to add nothing is possible with god, everything has to do with us. Sometimes I don't get it why us humans are hard on ourselves, instead of crediting our successes and hard work we will rather take away this credit and freely give it to the invisible being. It is us who are destroying this earth and life. In turn, it will be up to us to build this earth and preserve and nurture life by practically applying ubuntu. We should reduce or eliminate all the anti-life obstacles that were made by us.

Ubuntu appreciates the value of life. In ubuntu, no one will be going to sleep with an empty stomach. Someone's child is your child too. In ubuntu, the following are derogatory words: *orphans*, *street kids*, *stepchild*, *refugees*. According to ubuntu, these words are abstract they have no practical meaning because the community is there to take care of the so-called orphans. As a consequence of this, there will be no orphanages all the children who lost their parents will not feel isolated, and the home environment due to them will continue.

The streets of our cities will be free of the homeless, and we will only be dealing with trash, not young lives. This tragedy is endemic in the African cities, where it should have never existed in the first place. Are there no Abantu (people) to take them to the warmth of the family? I know many people have adopted the so-called orphans, and they continue to follow this compassionate trend. Whoever is neglecting and leaving these children to roam the streets is a topic for another time. If the ubuntu 'god' or ubuntu regime is in power, there will be no children roaming the streets of the big cities who might become vulnerable to abuses and indignity.

Individualism have consumed the sense of ubuntu. Selfishness has taken over the reins of compassion. Africa should regret not taking advantage of ubuntu and its simple basic tenets of togetherness. There is no heaven or Holy Spirit that will solve our problems. Let us all go back to basics of ubuntu. Ubuntu respects life.

Secular education

Since South Africa is a constitutional state founded on liberal values, such as rationalism, justice, diversity, tolerance, and scientific education, my proposal is that evolution should be a compulsory subject in South Africa from junior schools to the tertiary institutions. The University of the Witwatersrand (Wits) have what it takes to teach this subject; they should be tasked to work out this crucial issue by designing a syllabus to suit different grades of schooling.

We cannot skip evolution and pretend as if it is not there just to suit the believers. The state subsidy that is provided to universities, a portion that goes to faculties of theology should be diverted to the science faculties.

Since the religious institutions do not pay taxes though they are making profit more than some private companies, their faculties in universities and colleges that benefit from government subsidies should be excluded from receiving these funds. This is a waste of resources and time.

I wonder about the content of their thesis for their PhD. What type of a world are we living in if we can create faculties for lies and credit people with esteemed names, such as professors and doctors of theology? Are we not joking with the academic calling? When the world have been fully and perfectly secularised, these particular faculties and colleges would be a thing of the past. It is incumbent of the state to advance what is relevant today in the modern world in order to quell the diseases caused by beliefs in myths or to counter the dangerous beliefs that are detrimental to the society both in terms of attacks and psychological bondage brought about by the unproven ideas.

Firstly, secularism begin with *rationalism*. South Africa is founded on rationalism. Let me dissect this term *rationalism*. The main and the ultimate objective of the Enlightenment was the desire to release humankind from its bondage of superstition and ignorance and unleash the age of reason, which is the focal point of this book. Rationalism emancipates humankind from the grip of the past and from the weight of customs and tradition. Therefore, rationalism puts heavy emphasis on the capacity of human beings to understand and explain their world and find solutions to problems. Rationalism also emphasis principled and reason-governed behaviour as opposed to reliance on customs, traditions, and irrational drives and impulses. Heywood, 2013:27.

That is what we need more than anything in South Africa and the world today. Reason, moreover, is of utmost importance because of its emphasis on more engagement among human beings. This is the only path to avoid unnecessary brutal conflicts that characterises our part and are still raging in other parts of the world. Violence is the failure of reason.

The second requirement for a secular state is *tolerance* and *diversity*. South Africa is a plural society, meaning it has different cultures, religions, races, and so forth, much like the Western world today. All these different groups are expected to be loyal and be patriotic to South Africa. Unity in diversity—this is more beneficial than detrimental. Diversity cannot succeed without tolerance.

Firstly, this means we must tolerate one another. Tolerance is a willingness to allow people to speak, think, and act in ways that we disapprove. John Stuart Mill (1859–1972) said, 'Only within the free market of ideas will truth emerge, as good ideas displace bad ones and ignorance is progressively banished.' Heywood 2013:

30. If teachings of diversity had been carefully inculcated in the rest of the world, we would not be experiencing these wars over our differences today.

Evolution

Science has endowed us with the most precious gift that humanity has ever received—knowing our origins. I think we are the only species that know their origins. Where we come from, whether we accept it or not, is a fact of life it will never change. Truth will always be truth only lies changes because they have to be adjusted time and again to suit a particular situation and eventually be replaced by the truth. Truth is forever lies are temporary. There is no other explanation that will surpass this one.

After centuries of being bombarded with lies and inaccuracies about our origins as human species, science could not have come at a better time than this. Ancient men and women resorted to tales, fables, and legends to describe our origins. Unfortunately for them, there was no science to counter the tales with tangible evidence, which is not the case now.

Today science has put to rest the laughable story of Adam who never existed, who was apparently fashioned out of dirt by the hand of invisible being who never existed too and his partner, Eve, was ripped off from him, and they are falsely our forebears. All the indications and evidence are pointing to the mother continent of Africa. Of all places, South Africa should be the last country to entertain beliefs that claim to know the origins of humans since it is riddled with overwhelming evidence of our origins and of Africa being the original centre of humanity and particularly, South Africa being the cradle of humankind.

South Africa contains more hominids than any other place in the world. Sterkfontein in the west of Johannesburg was named by United Nations Educational, Scientific and Cultural Organisation (UNESCO) in 1999 as the world heritage site for being the centre of evidence of human origins. This is where the fossil museum is situated. Other fossils and discoveries are kept at the Origins Centre Museum in the University of the Witwatersrand in central Johannesburg.

Science tells us that we evolved from another life forms after millions of years of evolution. All the earliest evidence for hominids is found in Africa. Modern humans (Homo sapiens) appear to have evolved in Africa between 120 000 and 160 000 years ago. The hominid fossils dug in Maropeng and other parts of Africa and the world and the DNA analysis confirms this theory of evolution. As the science advanced, it became evident that we were more closely related to some of our fellow primates than previously imagined.

Microbiology has shown that we share approximately 98.4 per cent of our genetic material with chimpanzees and 97.7 per cent with gorillas; both are our closest surviving cousins in our big ape's family. In fact, DNA studies tell us that we are closely related to the African apes, with only about 2 per cent of our DNA different from theirs.

All these similarities have led scientists to believe that at some stage, we must have shared a common ancestor with the African apes. Esterhuysen, 2007:34.

South Africa and Africa are in abundance of prehistorical fossils. There is plenty of archaeological evidence to put to sleep any doubts about our origins. We should not be killing one another for imaginary crimes, such as witchcraft, and tie our minds to sins and life beyond the grave. Let's just live a simple life and feel for one another as ubuntu dictates.

Coping without belief

What are people going to do during Sundays and Saturdays? What about the gigantic architectural buildings and the theology colleges and faculties in universities? Many people are used to praying before meals, what will replace this? When tragedies and difficulties occur, people turn to god for salvation and comfort, especially when grief of losing loved ones befall the family. Many people are comforted and accept that the deceased is living in paradise with the Lord, where he/she is free from all the difficulties of the earth.

My countrymen and women who believe in ancestors do get solace when someone departs from this planet because they believe that the family or clan is waiting to welcome them with warm hands, and that makes the living persons accept the death of loved ones. If it happens that a child died, they would say he is staying with his great-grandparents and so forth. The idea that all of us are visitors on earth is well entrenched it is a comforting message to many people. Who will promise eternal life beyond the grave if beliefs disappear?

At the moment, people are busy going up and down all over the world, preparing for life beyond six feet. What will they do if they are told that their preparations are a waste of time and scarce resources? I also touched on hope as the ingredient that makes the beliefs useful. If the pious are told to forget about another life, their hopes will be hugely dashed. They would see no compelling reason to keep on believing. And that is our ultimate wish.

Living without belief may be the permanent solution, especially if we want to eliminate the belief crimes, such as killing the so- called witches, ritual murders, sectarian strife, and terrorism. These crimes emanate from the holy books, where the human trait of wickedness play its part, mostly figuratively in the book since the aim was to acquire unquestionable obedience. What really brought us here in this present situation is that the modern men took literally those horrific lines from the holy book and acted physically. The results speak for themselves and are clear and visible for all of us to see.

The unwritten religion is not immune too, it was passed down orally from generation to generation that the witch must be killed and her possessions pillaged. The other significant factor is psychological bondage, which causes enslavement of the mind and indebtedness to sins and inherent fear of the present life and the life beyond the grave. These mental factors can mean a lot in terms of freedom. Mind you, that freedom, if it is to be realised and be real must be the freeing of the brain.

We can demolish churches or mosques physically. Human nature has proved that it is not enough. These institutions must be demolished first from the head. Let us free our mind to face the real issues that are bedevilling us as humans. We have to deal with incurable cancers, AIDS, Alzheimer's, spinal injuries that are irreparable, poverty, scarcity of water, annihilation of the environment, and so on.

This is the main theme of the book. The removal of beliefs will not leave any vacuum that will need to be filled. I heard some commentators, even atheists, alluding to the gap that will be left open. Since beliefs are learned and not inherited, why would humans not survive after its demise. And why other humans are surviving without it?

Not all people believe

Not all people believe in witchcraft, especially in rural areas, where this is prevalent. There are few people I know both in rural and urban centres who do not believe in anything supernatural, the same as me. Some of them did not set foot in school. Just by pure reasoning, they refused to bow to magic influence. I found out about this not through research, it was just through spontaneous chats. Some fellows I know do not care whether there are witches, god, or whatever; they just enjoy life as it comes. Some Christians do not believe in the existence of witchcraft, but they do believe in the existence of the devil. Some of the ancestor worshippers asked the question, has anybody caught a witch? This means that even those practising traditional religion are not sure about the validity of witchcraft belief.

By the way, some of the so-called witch doctors, the traditional diviners, are devout Christians. They help both ways there is a time dedicated for Christian spiritual healing and a time for throwing bones and invoking ancestors when healing their clientele. They act as prophets and traditional diviners. They insist that both ways are not in competition but supplement each other in ensuring the health and future of the people.

CHAPTER 4

Combating belief crimes

Homophobia and sexism

Homophobia is regarded as unacceptable behaviour by the religious and traditional establishments in South Africa and the world. This hatred and the prejudice towards women is based or founded on the teachings of these institutions. Historically and naturally, culture, customs, and religion revolve around the men.

Why does the word *Queendom* not exist when queens have ruled countries for centuries? Even the queens did not bother themselves in changing this tradition. Why not *Herstory* instead of *history?* At least nowadays, some phrases have been brought in. It is rare to use the word *chairmen*; accommodating words or neutral words are used. *Chairperson* is used instead of the rigid word *chairman*.

These names and others point to our dark history of patriarchal dominance in every sphere of our society. Nowadays, this dominance is slowly losing its grip in democratic countries such as South Africa. But in theocracies such as Saudi Arabia and the traditional institutions here at home, the status quo is maintained.

It is even worse here in South Africa because the constitution has outlawed the discrimination against women, but the traditional leaders are intentionally brushing that away in the name of culture and tradition. They affectionately call themselves the guardians of African culture and traditions. Some of them even call gays rotten, and some advise the gays and lesbians to consult the traditional healers and witch doctors for treatment of this disease.

The African continent consists of fifty-four states. Out of this total number, only one country recognises same-sex marriages and relationships. This progress in South Africa is under threat from the above-mentioned institutions. Not surprisingly though, all their reasons in opposing gays and lesbians are based on rather hollow arguments. The fact that the holy books, which were written thousands of years ago, have passages that oppose homosexuality testifies to the fact of the presence of this phenomenon at the time when people were still wandering in the desert. It is unthinkable that the opposition of those men and the present men who oppose gays/lesbians and women equality was founded on non-scientific facts. The desert patriarchs had no science, whereas the present traditional leaders and men of the cloth have science in their midst. But their ignorance is one and the same.

The traditional leaders and politicians are very influential in the community. As a norm in South Africa, those highly esteemed leaders are disregarding the spirit of the constitution by uttering anti-gay messages and ridiculing gays, especially in public gatherings that are attended by throngs of people. Covered by the mass media, their incitement messages reach millions of South Africans in no time. The freedom of speech is guaranteed in the constitution, but to what extent is it allowed? The utterances are in direct contradiction to the bill of rights.

Homosexuality is enshrined in the constitution. This is an irony when considering that the same leaders who are supposed to preach tolerance and respect of the choice of others are sending an ugly message to the society. These messages are taken by some as approval to attack gays. We have seen the brutal killings of teenagers for being what they are, and the gruesome rape of lesbians by the so-called straight men who call it corrective rape.

Utterances such as *gays* are un-African. These utterances are sowing divisions among members of the society. Africa itself is reeling from years of civil strife and divisions that decimated her for centuries. Even now, in some sub-Saharan parts, tribal wars are incessantly raging. Divisions in Africa is the last thing in our list. These pseudoscientists (some traditional leaders, politicians, religious leaders, and laymen), who mistakenly think they know human anatomy and psychology, are constantly spewing lies and misleading the society by declaring that homosexuality is unnatural and that it is a crime against nature. Science has proven time and again and beyond reasonable doubt that the animal kingdom/queendom has its fair share of homosexuality. More than forty species of animals engage in homosexual behaviour.

But it is not all doom and gloom; there is some hope. The SABC (South African

Broadcasting Corporation) is airing soapies and stories starring gays and lesbians. These will help to familiarise the society with the prevailing situation. The traditional leaders are abdicating their core duties of protecting the senior citizens from witch hunters since most of the brutal attacks occur under their jurisdiction, meaning just under their noses whether they believe it or not. In this abhorrent belief, their duty is to make sure that nobody is killed in the name of this madness.

Rather than trampling on the rights of other citizens, their actions do not make any sense they should be preaching anti-witchcraft slogans. Old people are killed, maimed, displaced under their watch. Instead, what they do they chant anti-gay slogans.

Their umbrella body, known as CONTRALESA (Congress of traditional leaders of South Africa), is openly displaying its disdain of human rights and blatantly undermining the Constitution of the Republic of South Africa by proposing for the removal of gay protection from the bill of rights, which will adversely lead to criminalisation of gays and lesbians and will inadvertently lead to more attacks and the so-called corrective rapes. Their president is ironically a member of parliament and the ruling party that fought for and wrote the same constitution.

This traditional leader justified their anti-gay stance in a local Sunday newspaper by saying many South Africans do not support gays and lesbians. Interestingly, his own party ignores him to date. He forgets and ignores the fact that this is strictly a private and personal choice between two concerting individuals, a choice that does not hurt or disturb anybody the individuals enjoy their lives as they deem fit.

To our dismay, these guardians of African traditions and culture concern themselves with unproductive thinking and actions by spending their energy on what is happening inside people's blankets, who is sleeping with whom, and whether they're sleeping legally or not. I am not sure whether it is their business to even consider it. They support the anti-gay stance by citing African values and morals. God is also not left out of the equation they describe homosexuality as ungodly.

I don't understand. Maybe I am wrong. The last moment I checked, the killing of old people and the ripping of body parts from children were not African values and morals too and not godly either, but we have not witnessed this type of campaign and vigour that is directed towards gays and lesbians being waged against witch hunters and diviners. Is this is a way of building South Africa, by avoiding the real issues instead chase trivialities?

As I was born, bred, and schooled in rural areas, I know first-hand the challenges that our community is facing, especially the former Bantustan reserves, known as homelands. It is disheartening to see the people who must lead our areas to progress and much-needed development concerned themselves with bedroom issues of some adults. They should be equipping the rural schools with libraries and laboratories, replacing the mud schools, building the sewage system. Their subjects are sharing muddied water with the animals in the shallow dams and rivers, while they are busy chasing gays and lesbians.

Women too are not yet free because of entrenched traditions and beliefs. What else can block females from acquiring royal duties? There are many instances where the women who are supposed to occupy the throne are prevented from doing so due to their gender, some cases are pending in the courts of law. The Roman Catholic Church is refusing women top positions because of their gender and does not want to recognise homosexuals. This is not from themselves it is the holy book that prescribes it. Why blame them?

I think my case is very strong and convincing in that, by shedding off this unwanted burden called religion on our shoulders, more energy will be released for useful projects.

No ordinary criminals

The people who commit these gruesome acts are no ordinary criminals, they are not mad either. Yes, their deeds are criminal, but their motivation is what they have accepted, their beliefs/myths, with unwavering credulity. We must all acknowledge and accept this unfortunate reality. Are they running mad? No, the deeds are. Then where does this madness come from? It comes from their entrenched belief of believing in non-existent things.

By now, we all know that the consequences of believing or taking seriously something that is not based on credible evidence and thrives on irrationality are terrifying in magnitude. The terrorism that is sweeping the world by storm at the moment, especially in our dear mother continent, Africa is very terrifying. The direct targeting of civilians by Al-Shabaab in both Somalia and Kenya is gruesome and unimaginable. Killing people in restaurants of the battered Mogadishu, targeting shoppers in Nairobi, and killing sleeping students at Garissa University in eastern Kenya are the results of being magic minded.

Belief in the supernatural is rearing its ugly head. Al-Shabaab, like the Islamic State and Boko Haram and others who share their supernatural ideology, are not going to abandon their insistence on ruling the people with the dangerous and out-of-mind verses of the holy books. Their tactics on achieving what would never be achieved are costly in terms of human lives and the economics of the countries that they target.

People will never allow themselves to be ruled by the ideas that ruled more than 5,000 years ago. Even those theocracies that are ruling the Gulf States of the Middle East are ruling according to modern times at least. Otherwise, they would not have survived. There is a lot that have to be done by them in terms of gender equality, but the ideology of ISIS and Boko Haram will never work in the present world. They are just killing people for nothing.

Boko Haram, ISIS, Al-Shabaab, right-wing white supremacists, and killers of the so- called witches are all delusional. They all target innocent civilians by just shooting and bombing—sitting, eating, praying, and sleeping unarmed human beings. How can a twenty-two-year-old boy have the courage to hack a ninety-year-old granny and burn her alive? Because he thinks she is a witch. It can only be by being magic minded that they can afford such senseless brutality laden with bad ideas that emanate from religious ideas of putting faith before reason.

Why are we still sticking to the ideas that are leading us to oblivion? Can this be the clash of ideas? Yes, the clash of reason and unreason, the clash of modern and ancient times. What should have been a battle of ideas around the table has incorrectly shifted to a field dubbed the battlefield. Religion as an idea should be subjected to pounding like any other idea. Witch hunters and religious zealots are not ready to defend their ideas around the table, they would rather express them on the battlefield spilling blood, what else?

Solely blaming and criticising the perpetrators of violence, not what they stand for, is a futile exercise as it happened in the past. Those people are not just killing for the sake of killing; they fulfil the duty that is laid down by their respective beliefs. Before blaming the perpetrators of brutality, we must not leave out what really instigates them to be that bold and courageous in carrying out gruesome acts and justifying them.

The authorities should cease cushioning dangerous ideas and immediately implement laws that categorise the belief crimes as hate crimes and declare this silent crime as crimes against humanity as there is no justice in letting witch hunters get away with common murder. I know murder is murder; there is no better murder or worse murder.

This type of crime needs special attention. This special attention will pit the terrorists against the moderates, who always blame those terrorists for being extremists, not representing the entire faith, as if the extremists are from somewhere else it is just that the terrorists are implementing literally the whole text of the holy books. They have no tendency to pick and choose certain verses and omit others.

Banning false adverts

The South African government in 1999 passed the Tobacco Products Control Amendment Act. This act prohibits all advertisement and promotion of tobacco products. The act also restricts smoking in public areas. The act also stipulates penalties for transgression of the law. The regulations were implemented in 2001.

The Constitution of the Republic of South Africa (chapter 2, Bill of Rights, section 15) guarantees freedom of religion, belief, and opinion; everyone has the right to freedom of conscience, religion, thought, belief, and opinion. These rights are being abused by some churches by convincing people to abandon conventional medicine in favour of faith healing—laying of hands on the head and by selling them bottled water, holy oil, petroleum jellies—and fleecing money.

Again chapter 2 of the constitution of the republic of South Africa (Bill of Rights) comes to the rescue of the victims of churches. Section 36 (limitation of rights) stipulates the following: 'The rights in the Bill of Rights can be limited if this is reasonable and justifiable in an open and democratic society, that is based on human dignity, equality and freedom.'

The following are the factors that a person or a court must take into account if a right is to be limited: (1) the nature of the right (2) the importance of the purpose of limiting (3) how much can the rights be limited (4) the relation between the limitation and its purpose (5) the last one, whether there are better ways to achieve the purpose.

I can respond to factor number 2 here. The importance is the health of the people of South Africa. Their faith is being abused for the purposes of money, putting their health in jeopardy. The Department of Health in South Africa, as a custodian of the well-being of the society, is so far doing well. They encourage the nation to eat well, exercise, and stop smoking as preventative measures to illnesses. They have shown a keen interest in prolonging the life of the nation.

But all the successes that I mentioned above are being threatened by the new disease, a disease that is rather unusual. This disease is hell-bent on reversing the gains of the department. South Africa is recently experiencing the boom of bogus doctors, herbalists, pastors, and priests, who all claim to treat anything under the sun, even making debts disappear.

The main objective of the government act that I mentioned is to promote health and prevent diseases to protect the nation. Then, the authorities deemed it fit to intervene and save the nation; today that intervention is indispensable again. I request the Department of Health in South Africa to ban the false and misleading religious adverts that are risking the lives of unsuspecting believers. The ban should be a blanket ban on all forms of media with immediate effects.

They prey on the believers since they know that believers do not challenge anything from God. The devotees lured by these adverts on the most trusted national and regional newspapers are being unfairly misled to spend their hard-earned cash. These adverts encourage people to abandon scientifically approved, conventional treatments in favour of quick-fix miracles from God. This completely goes against the objectives of the Department of Health.

We are witnessing pastors selling bottled water and petroleum jellies as treatment for AIDS and other incurable diseases. The unregistered traditional healers and herbalist are also cashing in on unproven herbs and promoting vomiting as norms. They have been given a free rein for a long time. What is frightening is their daring advertisements on reputable newspapers.

These type of adverts are splashed out daily in print, online, on walls, on traffic lights. They use the unemployed to stand under the scorching African sun for the rest of the day and hand over pamphlets to passers-by and distribute them on heavily populated areas, like intersections, taxi ranks, and train stations.

These bogus pastors and herbalists are casting doubt on professional and proper medical treatment. South Africa is a country of many beliefs deeply embedded as they are, and we are a society with differing levels of education. There are documented and undocumented cases of people discarding proper medicine for bottled water from the church. The pastors and prophets are in a gold rush since many people are believers, the money just comes easy.

I don't know why they embark on this perilous journey unchallenged in broad daylight. Can it be that the liberal constitution is so accommodating to a point of allowing chaos? It seems as if we are in a banana republic people just do things as they wish because their sector of religion is the most protected and feared one. The authorities are reluctant to confront these herbalists, witch doctors, and pastors turned medical doctors due to the unfettered respect being given to religion, culture, and traditions.

These purported miracle treatments are aired on family television. Pastors are shown laying hands on the heads of the so-called sick, and all of a sudden, they stand up healed in a fraction of a second. The blind are treated to see after so many years of not seeing, those bound to wheelchairs are made to walk again, crooked legs are straightened up in no time to run again.

Maybe the authorities are afraid of being seen as not respecting God and his miracles or of being seen as intolerant towards religion. But I think religion and culture should not be allowed to be used for the wrong reasons, especially to jeopardise the health of the people and fleecing their money. The National Department of Health should summarily intervene to ban all the gimmicks on TVs, the dailies and weekend newspapers and online.

Some of us know that people are not healed by water and petroleum jelly. No pastors and prophets should be allowed to stage the treatment of people on the media and outside the media. An anti-faith-healing legislation should be introduced to curb the practice of misleading of the public through non-existent miracle healing. Nobody should be allowed to claim to have the know-how and antidote to treat incurable diseases, such as cancer and HIV. The way the authorities deemed it fit to ban tobacco advertisements to protect the citizens from harm of smoking must also be applied to these crimes of fraud.

Useless laws

The Witchcraft Suppression Act of 1957 was in force until it was repealed. Here I just quoted some of these ridiculous acts against the so called witchcraft. The act was against the following: the imputing on any other person, the causing by natural means of any disease or injury or damage to any person or thing, or the naming or indicating of any other person as a wizard. The sentence is ten years' imprisonment and alternatively a R400,000 fine.

The laws that suppress witchcraft were wide-ranging, there were offences which were deemed less serious. The sentences and fines were very lenient. This was another mistake that they made by separating and dividing one offence into pieces. The following offences attracted five years' imprisonment and a R200,000 fine: employing a witch doctor to find a witch or any other person, professing knowledge of witchcraft, using charms, advising a person how to bewitch others, infusing damage, supplying a person with any pretended means of witchcraft on the advice of a witch doctor or witch pretending to have knowledge of witchcraft. Lastly, pretending to exercise supernatural powers or witchcraft, tell fortunes, and find things which were lost or stolen.

This last offence is the one the authorities should be drafting legislation against. The wording is very accurate: *pretending to.* Yes, it can only be pretence, they are spot on. This type of offence summarises everything regarding the issue of supernatural problem-solving that is currently being employed by the rogue pastors and diviners, which are false, misleading, and dangerous its consequences involve leaving the victims dry in their pockets and filling the pockets of the offenders and, in doing so, encouraging supernatural thuggery. There is nothing that prohibits these types of crimes today in South Africa, as I stated in the chapter on media advertisements, where magic thugs claim to have the solutions to every problem experienced by human beings.

The drafters of the failed laws were wrong from the beginning. Firstly, they should have investigated the root cause of the problem before offering solutions. But it was not easy for them since they themselves were believers in supernatural powers and magic. I would be unfair to them if I entirely put the blame on them, they were also victims of invisible myth.

There is no better way to handle the situation other than the solutions that are always put forward by the secularists, which is ruthless secularisation. Any half-baked law drafted that will negate secularism to cushion the religious and traditional institutions will be a waste of time. When these laws are drafted, consideration must be paid to the nation and the constitution. The Constitution of the Republic of South

Africa is superior to religions and cultures, so everything the organised religions and cultural institutions do must be in compliance with the law of the land.

CHAPTER 5

Liberation from magic

Open-mindedness a road to atheism

In order to acclimatise one needs to be open minded. This is the very crucial part in the process of converting people from the magic-minded state into the evidence-minded state—a case of two extremes. There must be an opportunity of compromise, a mediating process. I myself became open-minded before choosing this alternative, but I have been a naturally open-minded person all along. What delayed me into becoming a secular humanist was my prevailing environment. There was no alternative to make a choice then. What is beneficial about open-mindedness is that you are free to approach any subject with an enquiring mind, critical thinking, and free thinking, meaning you do not just take things at face value.

The following quote put things into perspective;

> It is not so much that we are afraid of change or so in love with the old ways, but it is that place in between that we fear it is like being between trapezes. it is Linus when his blanket is in the dryer. There is nothing to hold on to. (Marilyn Ferguson, American futurist) Puth, 1996 127

Change is difficult. People fear change, but good communication can help ease the pain of change. As I said earlier, there has to be a no man's land, a transition. William Bridges, described transition as the psychological processes people go through to come to terms with the new situation Puth, 1996 127. Transition begins with letting go of something, then one has to understand what comes after the letting go, and that is where an area called no man's land is found between the old reality and the new.

This is the time when the old way is gone, and the new one does not feel comfortable yet. People can only make a new beginning if they have first made an ending and spent some time in the neutral. Our biggest mistake as secular humanists is that we start with the new beginning rather than first end the old. We must pay attention to endings and acknowledge the existence of the neutral zone; this would eliminate the obstacles that block the road from belief to unbelief. Changes and endings go hand in hand. Change leads to transition, and transition starts with endings. A new beginning can only be made once you have made an ending and spent some time in the neutral zone. This is the main ingredient for changing from a particular stance to another.

How can open-mindedness transfer people from believing myth to believing facts? How can this be achieved? This is a very urgent issue. Firstly, to be open-minded is to be open to criticism and to have a desire to learn more, know more, argue more, read more about different dogmas, one must not rely on what you have heard about them. Be a free thinker. You must have an immense passion to enquire. You must rely on what you yourself have found out.

I will outline a clear example to you just to outline what I really mean by being open. In South Africa the colonisers used to use derogatory words to call Africans. Well they thought so but in reality, those words are not derogatory in their true sense or literal meaning. The most common are *Kaffir* and *Bantu*.

The word *Kaffir* is an Arabic words that is mostly used in religious connotations, meaning person who is ungodly and not different from an atheist. People who are ungodly are found from race to race, tribe to tribe, etc. Even among those who used this word on Africans, some of them presumably were not believers even if they hid that in other words they were Kaffirs too. The meaning of the word has nothing to do with race. Owing to the fact that people are not open-minded, the word has taken this route. Not believing in a god is not limited to blacks even at that time of the colonisation. The literal meaning of the word has got no offence whatsoever— perhaps its symbolic meaning. But all in all, the word is wrongly used, and we have just accepted that. Because we just take what we are told, we do not enquire critically—that is, applying open-mindedness.

The second example is just as simple as you pronounce it. They called us the

Bantu(s) bracketed s is added as plural, meaning 'the people' just omitting the prefix, capital letter *A* (*Abantu* in Nguni languages). The main objective of the word was discrimination. The colonisers thought that if they referred to us as the people, they will be recognising us as worthy of life or being treated as people like them. So to fulfil the mandate of segregation, it was deemed appropriate to borrow an indigenous name and call us Bantus (Abantu, people/humans). They regarded this as derogatory of course, not understanding the real or literal meaning of the word or erroneously doing it intentionally. Now some of the present generation still regard this nice word as an insult because we just accept what we are told, not bothering to find out the truth for ourselves. This allows one to check facts or separate truth from lies or vice versa. Open-mindedness is some sort of neutrality, gauging the situation before making any move.

Well now, here is another tragedy. The enlightened ones also fall to this trap of not being open they too add to stereotypes that are prevailing among our modern society. Please pay attention to this dreadful and bizarre explanation being presented by the sector that is supposed to lift us from the dark cave to the nearest brightest star. I am referring to the *Oxford South African Pocket Dictionary* (third edition), 2006: where they give the meaning of the above widely stereotyped words: *Bantu*, (1) a large group of peoples living in central and southern Africa, (2) 'the group of languages spoken by these peoples'. This (Abantu) name refers to all that is human, one can not say a certain group living somewhere, and languages they spoke, these people are not speaking bantu, there is no language called bantu. The Abantu (humans) the dictionary is referring to who reside in Central and Southern Africa, are divided into clans and tribes with different languages and cultures.

These diabolical explanations smell of being close-minded (stereotypical) and not doing their homework of consulting the Abantu (the people) themselves to furnish the right details. Abantu (humans) living in Europe, Asia, and America or anywhere in the world are called Abantu (plural) Umuntu (singular)in Nguni languages. For fairness, I do commend them for the good explanation about the usage of the word at the bottom of the two wrong explanations. The Oxford dictionary says that *Bantu* is an offensive word in South African English when used to refer to individual black people. Considering that this dictionary is used by millions of South Africans, especially those who do not have English as their first language (I myself included in this category), the aspiring young people will grow up learning the wrong things if the status quo of stereotyping is being advanced by the learned.

This brings me to a very important subject—that is, the stumbling block in the world yesterday, today, and probably tomorrow if we do not take into cognisance the power of being open-minded and That is stereotyping. Stereotyping should be discarded or shed off before crossing over to the other side, the process I mentioned in the foregoing paragraph on transition.

Stereotyping is 'the process whereby we categorise people or events according to similarities that we perceive them as having'. Gibson & Hodgetts, 1991; 92. Stereotyping consists of three steps. First and foremost is that we identify categories by which to sort people; that can be race, sex, etc. Secondly, we associate attributes with those categories; they can be athletic ability, occupation, etc. Last but not least, we usually infer that all people in certain categories take on the attributes we have decided on (e.g. all blacks are athletic). The writer of this subject went on by saying stereotyping simplifies reality. I can add to that by saying it not only simplifies reality, but it dwarfs it.

These rigid human characteristics are hell-bent on maintaining the status quo. The world today could have been or can be better off without this anti-change phenomenon. Bloody wars have been fought. Stereotyping is not good at all because it makes people insensitive to one another. If a certain tribe or race is killed, other people will celebrate, insisting, 'Yes, they deserve to die. They are our enemies.' Such utterances are in direct violations of humanity, and these are the signs of stereotyping. Stereotyping is the synonym of the word *labelling*. Once a certain human is labelled, derogatory words are employed in name-callings.

A catastrophe is unfolding. We have just witnessed it here in South Africa in April 2015 (this year). We thought that those were things of the past, but how wrong we were. Stereotyping started when our African brothers embraced our shores. Name-calling was the order of the day. After a long time, those names were regarded as true and right. Then stereotyping reared its ugly head, and xenophobic attacks started. We also saw in 1994 what happened in Rwanda, where more than 800,000 people were hacked to death within four weeks. It started with labelling and name-calling. Some people were referred to as cockroaches, which needed to be removed. That was the start of the genocide.

Slavery thrived, opportunities were denied to others, humans trapped other humans in poverty, ideologies were created, sectarian strife bolstered almost every malice. Today that which constantly consumes humanity is linked to stereotyping. The witches are old females is another example of stereotype, because they are always usual suspects in witchcraft activities more than any other age group in the society.

But there is hope; it is not all doom and gloom. Let's just open our minds. Let reason judge what is being presented in front of us. Let us all leave reason alone to fulfil the mandate that nature intended it to perform. I assure all of you the results will be great. Where does stereotyping obtain its strength and legitimacy from? and it is able to last this long in our lives in spite of the advances in science and our own reasoning that are supposed to eliminate it? Stereotyping blinds us to not see the real world; it makes us always possess some foregone conclusions about anything, especially our fellow species.

The following quote do fit this subject:

> People do not to see the world as it is, but only as they expect it to be, in other words they see it through the veil of ingrained beliefs, opinions and assumptions. Heywood, 2013

Then what made people not see the world as it is? The answer is very simple. It is a cruel system designed to render human reasoning redundant—that is, nothing other than indoctrination. The main and ultimate objective of this system is to annihilate the capacity of human reasoning so that it can get a smooth landing and survive. Well, by now, I think almost all of us know it very well that when reasoning goes to sleep, only catastrophe would be awake. Then when reasoning wakes up again, the catastrophe runs away and goes to sleep. That is the main task of indoctrination. Evolution was to endow us with reasoning. Reasoning is the jack of all trades. What is advantageous here is that all of us humans are born with this gift except in cases where there is some sort of deformation. But all human beings have this gift. Then this question might appear: if this is true, why is the world in this manner today? People are committing genocide on an unprecedented scale and gross abuse of the rights of both animals and humans just for petty reasons such as colour, language, creed, tribe, and sex.

I think all this malice cannot be blamed on the lack of reasoning; there is no such thing, as I've stated. The problems we see and experience today I can say are due to our reasoning capacity. How do we exploit this gift that evolution endowed to us? It is not uncommon to hear somebody saying to somebody his/her reasoning capacity is low or poor. That is the main obstacle we are facing. We do not use our reasoning capacity to its maximum capacity, meaning 100 per cent performance or full use of it. Most of the time, this precious gift is redundant it is resting. I do not understand why we rest the gift that could take us to the higher levels of life and prosperity.

What is blocking us from implementing the full work of reason? In reality, faith is the enemy of reason because of its founding doctrine of unquestionable authority. The enemy of reason is indoctrination, which produces stereotyping. Indoctrination brutally suppresses reason it deprives it any space of manoeuvring. Since indoctrination will never lie down without a good fight, what is next for us as humanity?

Education can come to our rescue because secularisation will not be possible without a good and relevant education. In fact, secularisation is the education itself because of its founding principles of open-mindedness, rationalism and freedom of choosing. Secularisation does not provide any authority it is a free entity. This confirms that if reasoning can be entertained in all sectors of the society, we can proudly and safely wave a goodbye to all beliefs. That would be a new dawn to the world, and this could mean minus one of the products of stereotyping backed by indoctrination.

This would now present us with ample opportunity to face other monsters that are the product of stereotyping backed by indoctrination. These monsters are also refusing to bow down to reasoning. They are racism, tribalism, sexism, homophobia, and xenophobia. These social ills would not have succeeded without consistent bombardments on the minds, particularly the young ones, with dangerous and unproven ideas which always emphasise our superficial differences. We see humans tearing at one another because they do not look the same or speak the same language or because they practise different creeds. The subjugation of women was made into a culture. But big thanks to feminism, that is now beginning to wither away. By just opening our minds, our beloved planet that gives an abundance of life can be better off for all of us and the coming generations.

There is a well-known South African poet who is known for praising struggle heroes in our land and abroad. He said, 'An injury to a mind is an injury to an individual, An injury to an individual is an injury to the nation.' That is my take on embracing open-mindedness.

Religion-free generation

The second point of call is the state. The state invests in reason—meaning 100 per cent separation of state and religion—but that's not what is happening at present instead there is only partial separation. Full separation can only begin in earnest the day when all religious entities are taxed and listed under the Companies Act to tap on that free profit they acquire by doing nothing (free money), when there is total ban of religion in the public sphere, and when religion is regarded as a private entity.

The second solution will be the parents/ community. If the state by default is not leaning to any dogma, this will eventually translate to the community/parents. They will be able to raise religion-free offspring. When the prevailing culture is unbelief, obviously the young ones will have no belief, especially in the supernatural one, where will that belief be learned from if the state, parents, and society lack such instruments? Rationalism can be the order of the day if the land mass is littered with laboratories, libraries, museums, and space exploration centres.

In South Africa, my place of birth and residence, we are unfortunately blessed with countless beliefs. They include beliefs in ancestral spirits, Islam, Christianity, Hindu, Judaism. I only listed the major ones that have an influence on the state and the populace, but the others not listed also count. Obviously, these beliefs represent goodness according to their followers, and naturally, the opposite of good is evil, that being represented by Satan and witches.

If you were born, raised, nurtured, and schooled in the world I have dubbed as magic minded, then it goes without saying that the above-mentioned beliefs and their two sides—the bad and good—are ingrained in you. If you believe in Christianity, that will make you believe in the existence of witchcraft, especially if you are in Africa, because their basic survival mode is one and the same—the supernatural or the magic-minded people Harris, 2006: 89. Without this supernatural magic, both beliefs are dead. Contrary to this, if you were born and bred in the world of reality (that is, you are evidence minded), it would not be possible for you to believe any of the above-mentioned beliefs, even one that purports to represent the good. The religion-free generation will not be inclined to believe in any dogmatism whether representing the good or evil because they have been groomed with facts not fables.

The state vs beliefs

Let's face it, religions and traditional institutions still wield a sizeable amount of influence around the world, whereas they are not in power, excluding theocracies such as Iran and the oil-rich Gulf States.

I am referring to the secular constitutional democracies found in the northern hemisphere and few in Africa. These are made by the fact that the masses still believe in God and ancestors. They are the potential voters who have power in their hands to enthrone or dethrone their respective regimes.

Considering this state of affairs, it would be a political suicide for any regime that seems to be in contempt or intolerant of religion or culture or both. I do not think there is any democracy in the world that will dare to insult culture and religion. In South Africa, the constitution guarantees religion and cultures chapter 2, section 15. The drafters of the constitution had no choice but to agree with the masses to include the beliefs and cultures otherwise, they would not have tasted political power. Of course, their journey to power was not about the beliefs, but they could not have omitted it either. This includes all political formations; the opposition parties known for robustness and sometimes going overboard will never risk their paltry and fragile share of the electorate by openly challenging religion.

In South Africa, the political parties, both ruling and opposition parties, unite when addressing the members of the churches. Some churches do invite them collectively or individually, especially when the voting campaign is in full swing. It is advantageous to the politicians to address church gatherings they all sing one chorus for God, present themselves as servants of God, pledge in front of the pastors to work under the guidance of the Lord when ruling the nation, and conveniently lie and present false promises of looking after the concerns of the congregates, such as abortion and homosexuality, even though they know that the constitution is unambiguous and clear in proclaiming the legality of these two private matters that involve individuals concern.

Since the politicians realise that the sizeable number commanded by the religious institutions is unrivalled, they will be afraid to go against their expectations by applying complete secularisation. Even the established democracies, such as the United States of America, are not immune to this problem. In the United States, the pious wants to see the choice of being gays and lesbians and having abortion outlawed. Fortunately, the supreme court of the United States of America has ruled that gay and lesbian marriages are legal. Reason has prevailed, and the ancient beliefs are slowly losing grounds.

The motivation behind this is their beliefs. This means if the belief was not there, the court battles would not have taken place. There are those Christians in America who want to see the Ten Commandments displayed in public spaces. Considering that America is a multicultural and plural society, this religious short-sightedness is just to create problems than solutions. If only one religion is displayed in public places, this will be no be different from a theocracy, which America cannot afford to be.

All of us in the world, by now we should be moving towards secularism. In South Africa, Christianity is the major religion, like in most of Western countries. The public holidays that are official are Christian ones. At the same time, South Africa proclaims itself as a secular state based on constitutional democracy in which all religions and cultures can be practised and are treated equally but their actions speak the opposite. This has developed the sense that Christianity is the official religion of South Africa.

The state is also promoting beliefs by inviting prayers from all religions in government ceremonies. This is not needed religion should be a private practice. As we speak, the South African Law Reform Commission is investigating the possibility of taking out the one-sided religious holidays in our calendar. This is a good initiative. I hope they succeed. That would be a step forward for the incumbent regime in terms of levelling the playing field. They have left the issue for a very long time.

The pious masses must regard this as the best thing that can ever happen in terms of respecting the constitution and they must remember that every member of the society, whether they have a faith or not, is accommodated. These holidays have been celebrated for a very long time. I know many people in South Africa respect the constitution, and most of the time, they blast the ruling party and its leadership for deviating from the law of the land. I expect them to stick to that when the ruling party is implementing the constitution by removing the one-sided religious holidays on the South African calendar. I wish they will not be blamed for adhering to the constitution since they are always blamed for not adhering to the law of the land.

Conclusion

Witches will still fly in the minds of Africans as long as Jesus, Muhammad, god, ancestral spirits, Moses, satan and witchdoctors/ diviners are still operating in their minds, witchcraft will be in full force. Disappointingly, our free and independent media has willingly joined this magic movement by helping them to spread their wings of magic through advertisements of witchcraft cures on a daily basis. My wish is to end all that is not beneficial to the advancement of humanity.

Our government is repealing all the laws that failed to dislodge one half of the problem those ineffective laws that failed were aimed at taking out a belief from within a belief. A better strategy will be to secularise the nation, like Western Europe has done. Our country and continent have suffered so much under the inconsiderate past regimes. Now when we think the time for eating the fruits of the imperfect liberations is upon us, supernatural madness took over with a vengeance through terrorism and continued through witchcraft belief.

These twisted soldiers of the revered god of the desert, Boko Haram, Isis and Al-Shabaab are throwing into tantrums the fragile democracies and are deepening the crisis in the already bleeding nations. The heavy burden of worshipping two deities (ancestral spirits and the god of the desert) and simultaneously chasing away two wicked beings (the devil and the witch) have weighed heavily on the side of magic thinking.

South Africa could have been a better place if the ancestral spirit and god were working or were true in existence. Instead it is the opposite. I will refer to the South African and African situation. The most poverty stricken, the most consumed by the disease, the most prisons filled, the most unemployed, the most affected by crime, and the most uneducated are black South Africans, yet they are the most pious, worshipping two sides of the coin.

Reasonably god and the ancestors should have come to the rescue of their fellow subjects by now. Just forget about apartheid as the cause of these ills. Even apartheid itself could not have landed if god and the ancestors are true and in existence as givers of life and saviours of humanity. The real caring God would not have kept the brutal African dictators for years in power, allowing them to kill their own citizens through starvation, civil strife and constantly eliminating their opponents, creating a charity case for the world.

The real god with those attribute he is being credited with could have ensured that all his creatures are living in harmony, not at the mercy of brutal African kings and presidents. This is the crystal-clear example that there is no such being. Why are the African dictators not afraid of him or just respect him by ruling his creatures with compassion?

Secular humanism and ubuntu could not have come at a better time for the much-needed rescue and relief. Give simple life a chance. Let the voice of reason to be louder.

References

Esterhuysen, A.B. 2007. *Sterkfontein: Early Hominid Site in the 'Cradle of Humankind'*. Johannesburg: University of the Witwatersrand Press.

Harris, Sam, 2006. *The End of Faith: Religion, Terror, and the Future of Reason*. The free press publication.

Asante, M. & Mazama A. 2009. *Encyclopaedia of African Religion 1*. Sage Publications.

Daily Sun newspaper, May 30 2015. A flying visitor.

Niehaus, I. Mohlala E. Shokaneo K. 2001. *Witchcraft, power and Politics in South Africa*: Exploring the occult in the South African Lowveld. University of Chicago Press.

Heywood, A. 2013. *Political Ideologies*: political ideologies an introduction third edition. Palgrave Macmillan publishers.

Puth, G. 1996. *The Communicating Manager*. Pretoria, J.L. van Schaik Publishers.

Gibson, J. W. & Hodgetts R.M. 1991. *Organisational Communication: A Managerial Perspective*.

The Guardian [online newspaper], March 12 2012.

The Sowetan newspaper, April 4 2015. The village of Witches.

The Sowetan newspaper, May 20 2015. Priest Confesses.

<www.gov.za>, Constitution of the Republic of South Africa.

<www.unicef.org>, 2012. Report: African Child Witches.

<www.iheu.org>, 2009. Report: Witchcraft in Africa.

Wikipedia. Anders Brevik, tobacco ban

Sunday World newspaper, May 10 2015. Witchcraft cure advert.

Oxford South African pocket Dictionary third edition, 2006. Definitions.

Printed in the United States
By Bookmasters